A Guide to
Mountain Bike Trails
in Illinois

A Guide to Mountain Bike Trails in Illinois

Walter G. Zyznieuski and
George S. Zyznieuski
With a Foreword by Mike Ulm

Southern Illinois University Press
Carbondale and Edwardsville

Library of Congress Cataloging-in-Publication Data
Zyznieuski, Walter.
  A guide to mountain bike trails in Illinois / Walter
G. Zyznieuski and George S. Zyznieuski : with a
foreword by Michael Ulm.
      p.   cm.
  Includes bibliographical references.
  1. All terrain cycling—Illinois—Guidebooks.
2. Trails—Illinois—Guidebooks. 3. Trails—
Illinois—Maps. 4. Illinois—Guidebooks.
I. Zyznieuski, George, 1961-   . II. Title.
GV1045.5.I3Z99 1997
    796.6′3′09773—dc21   97-2190 CIP

ISBN 0-8093-2144-0 (cloth : alk. paper)
ISBN 0-8093-2145-9 (paper : alk. paper)

This book is

dedicated to

all mountain

bike riders

who enjoy

the outdoors

and the

adventure of

trail riding.

Contents

Contents

Illustrations

Foreword

I remember pedaling my way through the early seventies as a teenager on a well-worn Huffy Stingray. My friends and I spent countless hours riding our bicycles over every inch of our neighborhood. Much of our riding consisted of "peeling out" in gravel driveways, seeing who could leave the coolest skid marks in the street, and just riding to the candy store and between our houses. When we tired of these activities, we built ramps to jump with our bicycles and had contests to see who jumped the farthest or the highest. I had it made in this respect, since the ditch in front of my parents' house had a well-worn path through it leading to a perfectly graded ramp onto our gravel driveway. For years, the only way I arrived back at my house was with a flying finish out of the ditch.

As our riding skills increased, we began to expand our horizons. Every vacant lot, wooded area, and open field in our neighborhood became fair game for our bicycling adventures. Since we lived in the flat lands of central Illinois, hills and jumps were highly sought commodities and the trails that offered the wildest rides were the most popular.

After years of riding trails and jumps and learning how to control my body and my bicycle, I began to encounter a new challenge: failing equipment. My old Huffy Stingray could not endure the paces I put it through. I remember going through innumerable tires and inner tubes, bent handlebars, broken spokes, cracked forks, and the worst (and scariest) of all, a broken frame. My father stayed busy helping me make repairs. Once, he even had a friend of his braze my Stingray frame back together with an extra support brace. Every time I broke something on my bicycle, I wished that someone would build a better bike.

Toward the later seventies, I retired my Stingray for

a ten-speed road bike and my driver's license. Still, I yearned to ride trails, so my ten-speed became an off-road bike. Although the ten-speed was not nearly as agile as the Stingray, it did have different gears that made climbing hills much easier. Again, I wished that someone would combine the best of a ten-speed with the agility of a stingray. Further, if they made all of the components nearly indestructible, then you would have a great trail bike. Apparently, I was not the only person pondering this idea.

The first time I saw a mountain bike was an advertisement in the back of an early eighties edition of *Outside* magazine. They called this bicycle a Stumpjumper, and it looked like the bicycle I had been dreaming of for years. Eventually, I saved enough money, bought a Stumpjumper, and began to ride trails again. Sometimes, those childhood dreams come true after all.

Since their inception, mountain bikes have done nothing but grow in popularity. The appeal of bicycling, combined with the allure of exploring trails, has created one of America's most popular outdoor recreations. Most riders know about the trail-riding opportunities in their own communities. However, exploration is an important aspect of mountain biking. Riding new trails, enjoying the scenery, and discovering new places are all part of mountain biking's appeal. As this book shows, there are plenty of trail-riding opportunities around Illinois.

Walt and George Zyznieuski have done an outstanding job of researching trails across Illinois. Their hard work will improve your mountain biking enjoyment. Use this book as your guide to new adventures. Read about new trails to travel; then go exploring! Soon, you too will discover why mountain biking has become so popular.

See you on the trail!

Mike Ulm

Acknowledgments

We would like to thank a few people who helped us write this book. First, thanks to Mike Ulm, director of the Illinois chapter of Rails-to-Trails, for helping us identify trails that are "mountain bike compatible" and for providing us with up-to-date trail information. Thanks also to Bob Hargis and Chuck Ostreich, board members of Rails-to-Trails, Marty Buehler, former board member, and Bob Thornberry, of the Illinois Department of Natural Resources, for maps and updates on trails.

Thanks to our mom and dad for letting us use their home on weekends as a base to work from while we rode the trails in the Chicago area. A great bed, shower, and mom's home cooking kept us going through the day! Thanks also to our dad for helping us shuttle our vehicle to the end of some longer one-way trails. Thanks to Mary, Lindsay, and Tiffany Anderson for watching Nicholas and keeping him entertained while we entertained ourselves on the trails. We also appreciated the company of Greg Feeny, who helped us break in and explore some of the trails and reviewed some trail descriptions. Thanks to Brian Allen for providing us with bicycle rules.

We would especially like to thank our wives, Deb and Laura, for helping create the manuscript and for being patient with us during our travels and while we stayed up late typing trail descriptions. And, lastly, thanks to Southern Illinois University Press for allowing us the chance to explore these trails.

Introduction

Today more than ever, people are riding mountain bikes for fun and sport. Their popularity is so great that mountain bike purchases account for the majority of bike shop sales. To satisfy this wave of enthusiasm, we decided to provide a book that covers mountain bike trails, or off-road trail biking, in Illinois.

This book was a natural outgrowth of our previous book, *Illinois Hiking and Backpacking Trails.* Since we have completed more than 800 miles of trails throughout Illinois, we are familiar with "multipurpose" trails throughout the state. Many of the trails in our hiking books are multipurpose and allow mountain bike riders on them, as well as hikers and horseback riders. Unfortunately, there are not as many trails for mountain bike riding as there are for other uses. Part of this may stem from the fact that mountain biking is a relatively new sport. The trend in mountain biking will, we hope, improve the trail opportunities in the future as we see mountain bike clubs, trail organizations, and individuals lobby for more trails and get involved in the planning of these facilities. Appendix A lists some mountain bike organizations for interested individuals to contact for more information.

We think it is great that organizations such as the Du Page County Forest Preserve District, Lake County Forest Preserves, and the Illinois Department of Natural Resources are opening up more trails to off-road mountain bike users, and we hope to see other parks follow suit. In parks where there are multipurpose trails, sharing has worked well and trail users are getting along. For example, while riding the trail at Argyle Lake State Park, we passed a horseback rider along the trail. Because he stopped to let us by, we greeted each other and talked about the trail. He said that he had no problems with the multipurpose status of the trail: we all pay for the trails, and so everyone should get a chance to use them. We second that opinion!

While we were doing our research, we discovered that there are numerous types of trail surfaces that mountain bikers can ride on, including dirt, mowed grass, limestone screenings, asphalt, old railroad beds, and roads. All of these trail surfaces are suitable for mountain bike riding although typically mountain bikers are not interested in asphalt or even limestone screened trails. Limestone screened trails and old railroad rights-of-way, generally, are level, crushed-rock surfaces.

For our purposes we included trails that consisted of both dirt and grass surfaces, as well as those that have limestone screenings. We included both trail types for two reasons. First, we have noticed a trend of individuals using "cross bikes," or bikes suitable for both street riding and trail riding. In fact, we used a cross bike on many of the trails in this book. Second, because there are relatively few dedicated mountain bike trails in the state, many riders are seen along these limestone screened trails.

One type of trail that we are seeing more of is old railroad rights-of-way. These trails make excellent mountain bike trails and a few of the trails listed in our book are converted railroad rights-of-way. In fact, one of the first rail-trails in the country, the Illinois Prairie Path, is included here. One of the newer rail-trail conservation efforts, the Tunnel Hill Trail, is located in the Shawnee National Forest. This trail is being developed by the Illinois Department of Natural Resources, and when it is completed, it will go through 40 miles of the forest. Approximately 11 trails listed in this book are rail-trails. For more information on rails-to-trails as well as other trail organizations, see Appendix B. In the future, new trail opportunities may be opening up along the many flood control levees found along the major rivers in Illinois.

We obtained information on potential mountain bike trails from many local, state, and federal agencies. If we have missed a trail suitable for mountain bike riding, let us know. As trail managers become more comfortable with mountain bike riders, more trails may be opened up to them in the future.

Always check with the park or trail organization for the current trail status. We did not include any trails in the Shawnee National Forest even though mountain bikers are riding trails in the forest. We did so for a reason. The Shawnee National Forest, in our opinion, is one of the most beautiful areas in the state. To help manage the Shawnee National Forest, a management plan referred to as the Amended Land and Resource Management Plan was implemented in 1992. The plan outlines proper uses allowed in the forest. According to a letter we received from the Forest Service in 1996, the current management plan allows mountain bike riding only on "hardened roads" in the forest. This is being loosely enforced until a new management plan is written. We hope the new plan will allow mountain bike riding on the trails. If and when the Forest Service opens up riding in the forest, long-distance trails are covered in *Illinois Hiking and Backpacking Trails*. Please contact one of the Forest Service offices listed in Appendix C to get some suggestions for which scenic roads to ride within the forest. The Forest Service also sells topographic maps showing the boundaries of the forest, as well as roads, contour lines, buildings, and the like. Contact the Forest Service or the United States Geological Survey in Appendix C for a list of the maps they sell.

Mountain bike riding can be hazardous. While the authors and publishers tried to help identify some of the risks associated with this activity, it is the rider's sole responsibility to identify and be aware of all potential risks and hazards associated with mountain bike riding. Use extreme care and know the risks before you decide to go mountain bike riding. You are responsible for your own safety.

A Note on Equipment

Everyone has heard over and over that an important piece of equipment to get is a helmet. We can't stress this fact too much since it has come in handy for us more than once—good protection when you fall off your bike or hit a tree branch. The bottom line is, wear your helmet!

Other equipment we normally carry includes a new inner tube or patch kit, tire pump, tools, water bottle(s), equipment holder or day pack, raingear, and various snacks. Every rider differs in needs and wants. A few books listed in the bibliography discuss equipment as well as maintenance of bikes.

The mountain bike trails we have included are located throughout the state on local, state, and federal properties. The main concentration of trails is in the Chicago area, but many of these trails are fairly short. The trails listed range in length from 3 to 78 miles. The longest trail described is the Hennepin Canal State Trail.

The adjacent map shows the location of trails by county. Each number corresponds to the number of the trail described in the book (a total of 48) and are arranged by location, from 1 in northwestern Illinois to 48 in the southeastern part of the state. We describe more than 655 miles of trails.

There is a map for each trail based on the U.S. Geological Survey maps and other sources. Many parks have detailed trail maps of their own, and so it may be useful to contact the park to obtain one. A word of caution, however. Some park maps may not be current and many trails may be closed or shown incorrectly. In addition, we did not include all roads and other connecting trails on our maps. Many times there may be connecting hiking or horse trails that are off-limits to mountain bike riders. We drew only the multipurpose trails on the maps.

Trails range in difficulty from extremely easy to challenging, although a typical Illinois trail is nothing compared with a mountain bike trail in the Ozarks or in a western state. Moreover, trails may or may not be marked with signs, blazes, or trailboards. We describe how each trail is marked in the trail description. Some of the trail information and park history was obtained from the park brochure.

Since there are so few mountain bike trails in Illinois, it is imperative for bikers to respect the trails in existence. This means that we should all stay on the

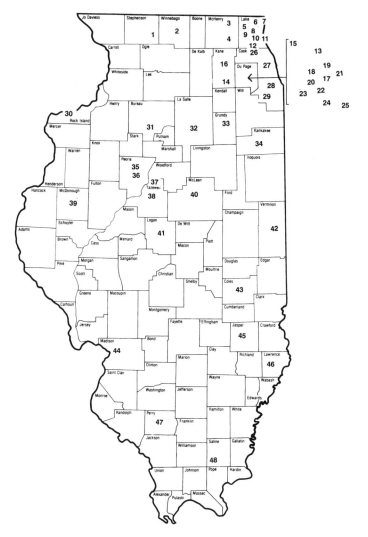

Mountain bike trails in Illinois

designated trail and riding surfaces and not stray off and blaze trails of our own. Trail blazing may lead to a ban of mountain bike riding at a particular park and may also do environmental damage. Respect your trails! (See Appendix D for rules of the trail developed by the International Mountain Bicycling Association. In addition, see Appendix E, Bicycle Rules of the Road. Appendix F includes information on the proposed Grand Illinois Trail, which the Illinois Department of Natural Resources is promoting. This trail will stretch over 475 miles in northern Illinois, once completed.)

We hope that you enjoy one of the trails listed in this book, and maybe we'll see you along the trail.

A Guide to
Mountain Bike Trails
in Illinois

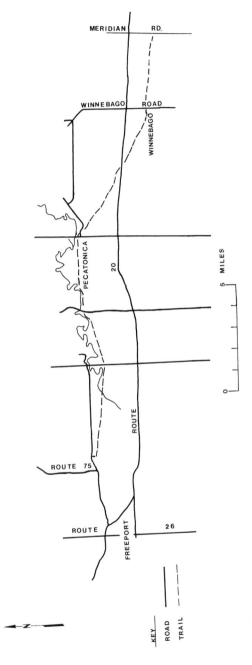

Pecatonica Prairie Path. Redrawn from Illinois Department of
Transportation Highway maps.

1. Pecatonica Prairie Path

Trail Length: 20.75 miles, one way

Trail Surface: Crushed rock, dirt

Counties: Stephenson, Winnebago

Location: The Pecatonica Prairie Path is located in northwestern Illinois between Rockford and Freeport. The trail passes through Winnebago, Pecatonica, and Ridott and ends (or begins) at the eastern edge of Freeport, just east of the U.S. 20 Bypass. This is the westernmost point of the trail, which is at the junction of Hillcrest Road and East River Road. This trailhead is somewhat inconvenient because there is no trail sign or parking, and traffic on East River Road is high speed. Roadways leading to this westernmost point outside of Freeport include north-south Route 26 to Freeport, east-west Route 20, and the Route 20 Bypass.

A parking area is located in Winnebago, which is just south of Route 20, about 7 miles west of Rockford. From Winnebago Road go west on McNair Street to North Swift Street, then south to the trailhead (three blocks). Limited parking is available here, but parking is allowed at the Winnebago High School parking lot at the intersection of Winnebago Road and McNair Street.

A third access is located in Pecatonica at Sumner Park. From Pecatonica Road, turn west on First Street, the first east-west street south of the Pecatonica River. This access point is very convenient because it is at about the midpoint in the trail, and it provides adequate parking along with water and restrooms at Sumner Park.

Route 51 is a major north-south route leading to Rockford, and from the east the major roadway is Northwest Tollway I-90. From Rockford follow I-90 to Route 20 west to either of the three access points mentioned. The trail may be reached from several other north-south roads but no facilities are provided except the parking lot at Farwell Bridge Road.

Trail Description: The Pecatonica Prairie Path follows the old right-of-way of the Chicago and Northwestern Railroad, now owned by Commonwealth Edison Company. The path is leased to the Pecatonica Prairie Path, Inc., a nonprofit organization formed to develop and manage the path for public use. It passes through forests and villages, over rivers and creeks, past farms, and across highways. Caution is necessary when crossing Route 20 since this is a major four-lane highway. Other hazardous crossings include Pecatonica Road in Pecatonica and Rock City Road in Ridott.

Most of the trail is gravel and dirt and is very level; it is about 10 feet wide. Trailboards are located at major crossings and trail signs are seen along the trail. The undisturbed land along the undeveloped sections of the path provides an excellent refuge for a variety of wildlife. More than 60 species of birds have been recorded. Deer, badger, fox, and raccoon are also often seen.

The path parallels the Pecatonica River in an east-west direction, although the river is visible from only a few spots. Except at Ridott and Pecatonica, water and restrooms are not available along the path. There are, however, four shelters along trailside between Pecatonica Road and Hillcrest Road. These shelters offer a picnic table with a roof for sunscreen.

The newest section (3.75 miles) is east of Winnebago, from Elda Street to Meridian Road. This section passes through both light commercial and residential areas in Winnebago, past the water tower, and through residential and rural areas as it heads east. At Meridian Road the trail ends next to an oil refinery tank farm. There is no convenient parking at Meridian Road.

Facilities: No camping or restroom facilities are available on the path. Parking is available at Ridott, in Sumner Park, at the Winnebago High School parking lot, at the Farwell Bridge crossing, and along county roads. Water is available at Sumner Park. Restroom facilities are available at Sumner Park and in Ridott.

Park Rules and Regulations: No motorized vehicles are allowed. Bicycles must have bells to warn hikers and other riders. No firearms. No bows and arrows. No kite flying. No model airplane flying. All dogs must be on a leash. No alcoholic beverages. No fires.

Hours Open: The trail is open to the public year round. For safety, use it during daylight hours only.

Mailing Address and Phone Number: Pecatonica Prairie Path, P.O. Box 534, Pecatonica, IL 61063; 815-229-3453

Pecatonica Prairie Path trail sign

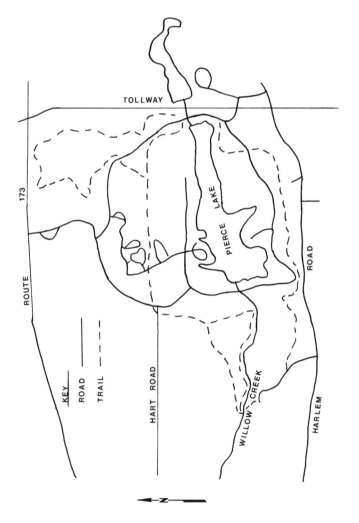

Rock Cut State Park. Redrawn from park map. Map not drawn to scale.

2. Rock Cut State Park

Trail Length: 9.5 miles

Trail Surface: Dirt, grass, rock

County: Winnebago

Location: Rock Cut State Park is located 7 miles north-east of Rockford. The park can be reached from the south via Route 51 north to Route 20. Follow Route 20 west and turn north onto Route 251. At Route 173, turn east and follow the road signs to the park. From western Illinois, the park is reached by Route 251 north from Rockford, again to Illinois 173 east. From eastern Illinois, the park is easily reached via I-90, the Northwest Tollway, to the Riverside exit.

Trail Description: The total area of the park is 3,092 acres. Rock Cut State Park reportedly was named for the abandoned quarry operations from more than a century ago. Evidence of old quarry pits are visible at the northeast shore of Pierce Lake. These pits are now filled with water and are rearing ponds for migratory birds and local wildlife.

   Good park maintenance is evident; all the trails are mowed in the grassy areas and kept clear-cut through the more dense areas. Foot bridges cross different waterways in the park.

   Pine Crest Picnic Area is a convenient place to start biking. Other convenient parking locations include the three separate parking lanes south of Hickory Hills Campground and the parking area located directly north of the dam.

   There are two main loop trails available for mountain bike riding identified as the Bike, Ski, and Hiking Trail (B.S.H. Trail). The shorter trail is easy to reach by parking at the Pine Crest Picnic Area and starting the trail at the eastern edge of the picnic area.

This 4-mile loop trail offers natural diversity, from open fields to moderately dense wooded areas, challenging hills, and wide lanes. North of the Pine Crest Picnic Area, the B.S.H. Trail is two-way; south of the park road and picnic area it is one way.

About 1/4 mile south of the park road, at Pine Crest Picnic Area, the western part of this loop, the trail meets at a T-intersection where you go east about 25 yards and then go south again. About an eighth of a mile down this wide lane the trail joins an inner loop hiking trail.

This section is a one-way trail (clockwise). An extremely steep hill is located just before heading south toward the lake. There are landscape timbers that are found while descending the hill; this section is not recommended for riding; rather the rider should dismount and walk.

The longer loop trail follows the perimeter of Pierce Lake and the park road, going by picnic areas and campgrounds.

At the southeast section of the lake, along the park road, there is a parking area near Lions Club Area. This parking area is convenient to ride the B.S.H. Trail west to the Willow Creek Area.

At the entrance to the Willow Creek Area, the trail system follows the asphalt road to the road's end. The trail then becomes a narrow path along the creek. You will then cross a ford over the creek and will come to a junction in the trail. During the wet season be careful crossing Willow Creek; the ford is a level concrete slab about 10 feet wide and nearly 20 feet long.

On the north side of the ford, the trail splits into an east and a west spur. The first spur meanders directly east along Willow Creek for one mile; the second spur passes through more dense foliage and at higher elevations. The second trail follows a ridge that overlooks a meadow, Willow Creek, and the first trail.

The two trails make a loop north of Willow Creek; at the trail junction the trail heads north. This additional section of the trail system meanders along the main park road for a quarter of a mile to Hart Road (gravel road going west). The trail goes directly east, passing by the camping and picnic areas, and then winds down to the park road by the northeast section of the lake and park road, joining the first loop at Pine Crest Picnic Area.

Facilities: Rock Cut State Park has five different camping areas with more than 215 class A sites. There are also five areas reserved for picnicking only. Tables, outdoor stoves, drinking water, pit toilets, and playground equipment are available. There is a shower building in the Plum Grove Campground and shelters at the Willow Creek Area. The park also has two sanitary dump stations.

The park is open for winter sports, including ice skating, ice fishing, cross-country skiing, snowmobiling, and dog sledding. Two fishing piers are accessible for the handicapped, and outdoor privies are available at the parking lots nearby.

Pierce Lake is annually stocked, and fishing is allowed with all Illinois fishing rules and regulations in effect. Boating is allowed on the lake, with two boat launch areas available. A concession stand is located at the boat launch area.

Swimming is available at the 50-acre Olson Lake located on the extreme east side of the park (north of the Harlem Road entrance and east of I-90).

Park Rules and Regulations: No plants or parts of any tree may be removed or damaged. The motor limit is 10 hp. All pets must be on a leash. Bicycles are not allowed on dedicated hiking trails. Do not ride when trails are wet or snow covered.

Hours Open: The park is open every day of the year except Christmas Day and New Year's Day. At certain times of the year, the roads may be closed because of freezing and thawing, and access to the park is by foot only.

Mailing Address and Phone Number: Rock Cut State Park, 7318 Harlem Road, Loves Park, IL 61111; 815-885-3311

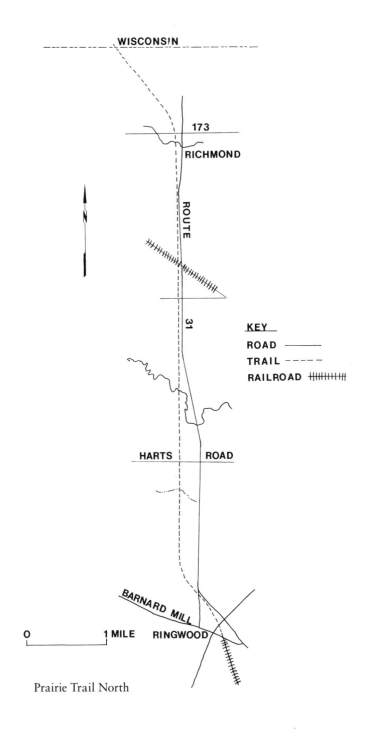

WISCONSIN

173

RICHMOND

ROUTE

31

N

KEY

ROAD ⎯⎯⎯

TRAIL ⎯ ⎯ ⎯

RAILROAD ▚▚▚▚▚▚

HARTS ROAD

BARNARD MILL

0   1 MILE

RINGWOOD

Prairie Trail North

3. Prairie Trail North

Trail Length: 7 miles, one way

Trail Surface: Old railroad grade

County: McHenry

Location: The Prairie Trail North is located between the city of Ringwood and the Wisconsin State Line. To reach the southern terminus, take Route 31 about 6 miles out of McHenry to Bernard Road in Ringwood. Turn west on Bernard Mill Road and go a short distance until you see the active rail line on the left side of the road. Park along the street in the general area and the start of the trail is to the right. Parking is also available at Harts Road, which is located 3 miles north of Ringwood. A small parking area is found just west of Route 31 along the west side of the trail. Bikers may also park in Richmond along one of the streets and begin the trail there.

Trail Description: The Prairie Trail North is an abandoned rail-trail that has been converted to a multipurpose trail by the McHenry County Forest Preserve. The trail's southern terminus is in Ringwood, and it goes north all the way to the Wisconsin State Line. Trail users allowed on the trail include bicyclists, hikers, horseback riders as well as snowmobile riders, weather permitting.

The trail begins near Bernard Mill Road in Ringwood and goes by a few commercial buildings as well as some homes. Past Ringwood, the trail goes under a wooden bridge structure and then it opens up to farmland as well as a marsh area. Some wooden benches are found in this trail segment and the trail goes over a few more wooden bridges.

At 2.3 miles, the trail crosses Hart Road, where the

Harts Road access, Prairie Trail North

parking lot is seen on the west side of the trail. A stair-
case leads you to the parking lot. Past this parking lot,
the bicyclist will shortly come to and cross Nippersink
Creek; a good view is had from the bridge. Soon it will
go by the Richmond High School football stadium,
some small businesses, and then the outskirts of Richmond. In Richmond, the bicyclist will go under a
wooden bridge and then go by an old church. A side
street can be taken into Richmond to stop in one of the
local establishments for a break.

The trail goes over the north branch of Nippersink
Creek, where a nice little waterfall is seen. Shortly after
the creek, the bicyclist will come upon Route 173. This
road can be busy; be careful when you cross this road.
The trail north of Route 173 is less urbanized, with
open fields and farmsteads. Within 2 miles, there will be
a Wisconsin State sign, and for all practical purposes,
the trail ends here.

Future plans call for extending the trail south from
Ringwood to connect with the Prairie Trail South segment and the Fox River Trail and beyond.

Sharing the trail, Prairie Trail North

Facilities: A picnic table and a garbage can are found at the parking area at Harts Road. Just west of the parking area, Glacial Park is located, where one can go hiking. (See *Illinois Hiking and Backpacking Trails.*)

Park Rules and Regulations: No motorized vehicles, except snowmobiles, weather permitting.

Hours Open: 8:00 A.M. until sunset

Mailing Address and Phone Number: McHenry County Conservation District, 6512 Harts Road, Ringwood, IL 60072; 815-678-4431

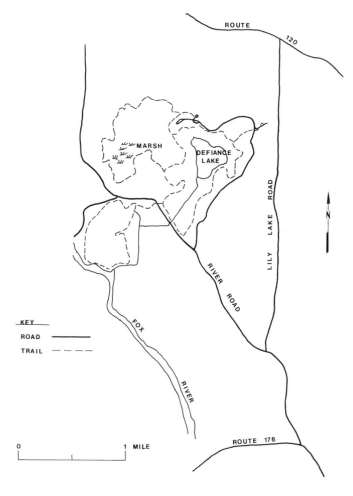

Moraine Hills State Park

4. Moraine Hills State Park

Trail Length: 10 miles

Trail Surface: Limestone screenings

County: McHenry

Location: Moraine Hills State Park is located in northeastern Illinois just south of McHenry. The park boundaries are centered between north-south Routes 31 and 12 and east-west Routes 120 and 176. From Route 176, turn north on River Road, and go 2 miles to the entrance; from McHenry and Route 120, turn south on River Road and go 3 miles to the entrance.

Other north-south roads that pass near the park are Illinois Tollway I-94, Route 45, and Route 47.

Trail Description: Moraine Hills State Park has 1,740 acres of upland and wetland environments. The rivers, lakes, marshes, prairies, and woodlands here are the result of the most recent glacial advance, the Wisconsin Glacier. At one time this area was occupied by several Indian tribes, including the Potawatomi, Sauk, and Fox.

Construction of the McHenry Dam on the Fox River began in 1934 after several land acquisitions in the area. Major land acquisition of the Lake Defiance area began in 1971. After a resource study and completion of a master plan, construction of the park facilities began in 1975.

The 10-mile trail system at Moraine Hills State Park consists of three main loops. The trail system is designed to be ridden one way only and is very easy to follow. From the Northern Lakes Day-Use Area, the Leather Leaf Bog Trail is located behind the comfort station, and the direction of travel is west (counterclockwise as you refer to the map).

Trailboards with maps and park rules and regulations are located at all day-use areas (parking lots). Trail signs are located at all trail junctions indicating the name of the trail, direction of travel, and mileage.

The Leather Leaf Bog Trail measures 3.5 miles and represents an excellent example of kettle moraine topography and supports very diverse plant communities. Plant species include marsh fern, marsh marigold, and willow.

The Lake Defiance Trail, which surrounds the 48-acre lake, measures 4 miles. It connects the Northern Day-Use Area with the Lake Defiance Day-Use Area and the park office. Along the Lake Defiance Trail is the concession and interpretive center. As the trail meanders southward, paralleling the park road, connecting trails allow access to several day-use areas—Hickory Ridge, Pine Hills, Kettle Woods, and Pike Marsh. At the southwesternmost point of this trail, there is a connecting trail going west under River Road. The connecting trail is for the Fox River loop, which is also designed for travel in one direction only.

The Fox River Trail passes through prairie areas adjacent to wetlands. A short trail leads to the parking area at McHenry Dam and to the concession area. The southern portion of this trail parallels the Fox River and the water drainage channel from Lake Defiance. The total length of this loop is 2.5 miles.

Additional hiking trails in the park are the Lake Defiance Self-Guided Interpretive Trail and the Pike Marsh Interpretive Trail. The Lake Defiance Self-Guided Interpretive Trail is accessed from the Northern Lakes parking lot and from the Lake Defiance parking lot to the park office, where the numbered posts begin. The hiking trail at Pike Marsh is accessed from the parking lot at Pike Marsh Day-Use Area.

The diverse landscape in this area of McHenry County provides habitat for numerous forms of wildlife. More than a hundred species of birds have been identified. The area is heavily used by mallard, teal, wood duck, Canada geese, and other migratory waterfowl.

Various mammals including red fox, eastern cottontail, mink, opossum, raccoon, and white-tail deer can be seen in the upland timber of oak, hickory, ash, cherry, dogwood, and hawthorn.

Facilities: Moraine Hills State Park has several parking areas. Picnic tables are available in all day-use areas, along with water and comfort stations. Picnic shelters are available at the Pine Hills and Pike Marsh Day-Use Areas. There are flush toilets at the McHenry Dam concession building and at the park office.

Playground equipment is available at the McHenry Dam area and at the Whitetail Prairie and Pike Marsh Day-Use Areas. Boats are available on Lake Defiance.

In addition to the concession at McHenry Dam area there is a concession at the park office. An interpretive center is also located at the park office.

Park Rules and Regulations: Groups of minors must have adequate supervision and at least one adult for every fifteen minors. All pets must be on a leash. There are no camping facilities available at Moraine Hills State Park.

Hours Open: The park is open year round except on Christmas Day. At certain times, because of freezing and thawing periods, the park is closed.

Mailing Address and Phone Number: Moraine Hills State Park, 914 S. River Road, McHenry, IL 60050; 815-385-1624

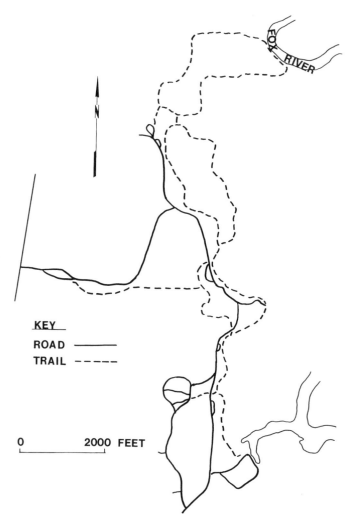

Chain of Lakes State Park. Redrawn from park map.

5. Chain of Lakes State Park

Trail Length: 7 miles

Trail Surface: Limestone screenings

County: Lake

Location: Chain of Lakes State Park is located in the northwest part of Lake County, just south of the Wisconsin border. To reach the site take Route 173 west out of Antioch. Follow Route 173 for 6 miles and turn south at Wilmot Road. Take Wilmot Road for 1.75 miles to the park entrance, where a park sign is seen.

Trail Description: The bike trail at Chain of Lakes State Park is a packed gravel surfaced trail about 8 feet wide, and it consists of three separate loops. It starts (or ends) at the gatehouse when you first come into the park, or it may be reached from other parking areas within the park. The trail is marked with mileage posts along the trail. It crosses the park road a few times, and stop signs are found at these road crossings.

   If you start the trail system near the gatehouse, the trail is known as the Cat Tail Trail. It parallels the park road, going by an open prairie area and through a small wooded area. This trail is a mile long, is marked in brown, and joins with the Sunset Trail, which is marked in orange.

   The Sunset Trail, 1.7 miles long, goes by a marsh and then a wooded area. A camera signpost is seen at a trail junction where a short trail takes the visitor to a platform overlooking the marsh where bird species like herons may be observed. The trail goes by the Pike Marsh North Area, where there are some picnic facilities, and also passes by the Oak Grove Picnic Area. At the south end of the trail, the boat launch area is found as well as the concession area. Boats, motors, and bicy-

Riders along trail, Chain of Lakes State Park

Rest spot along the Fox River, Chain of Lakes State Park

Viewpoint along trail, Chain of Lakes State Park

cles may be rented at the concession area. An information board describes the lake and the trail.

The next loop is the Badger Trail, which is 1.6 miles long. This trail segment is marked in white trail markers. The trail starts out going up a small hill where a picnic table is located. A nice view of the valley is seen here. The trail then goes down the side of the hill with a marsh area off to the right. At the north end of the trail the park office complex will be seen. The next loop trail, the Gold Finch Trail, is joined here.

The Gold Finch Trail is 1.7 miles long and is marked in yellow. It goes through a wooded area, by a stand of pine trees, a picnic shelter, and small ponds, and passes by the Fox River, where there is a good view of the river. Two picnic shelters are found at the river. The trail then goes uphill away from the river and past another small pond. Soon the Gold Finch Trail passes the Visitors Center, where the other trail loops lead you back to the starting area.

A great view of the floodplain can be seen from the Badger Trail just south of the Visitors Center.

Trail access, Chain of Lakes State Park

Facilities: Numerous picnic shelters are found throughout the park, as well as a campground, Visitors Center, concession, and a boat launch.

Park Rules and Regulations: All vehicles must be licensed and must remain on the road. Pets must be leashed. Swimming and wading are prohibited. Must be 21 to have alcohol. No firearms or hunting allowed. No gathering of firewood. No roller blades or skates or skateboards on the roads. Bikers must yield to pedestrians and stay on surfaced trails.

Hours Open: The park is open from 6:00 A.M. until 9:00 P.M. The camper's gate is closed at 9:30 P.M., with no reentry. The Visitors Center is open Monday through Friday from 8:00 A.M. until 4:00 P.M.

Mailing Address and Phone Number: Chain of Lakes State Park, 8916 Wilmot Road, Spring Grove, IL 60081; 847-587-5512

6. Des Plaines River Trail (Lake County), Northern Section

Trail Length: 8.3 miles, one way

Trail Surface: Dirt, limestone screenings

County: Lake

Location: The Des Plaines River Trail is located in northeastern Illinois along Route 41, just south of the Wisconsin border. The main trailhead at Sterling Lake is reached from Route 41, an eighth of a mile north of Route 173. A sharp right onto a paved road will lead to the parking area. The entrance to this parking lot may be closed at certain times of the year, depending on the weather. A second access point may be reached north of the main entrance off Route 41. Follow Route 41 north to Russell Road. Turn east on Russell Road, go a quarter of a mile, and turn south to the north entrance of Sterling Lake.

Trail Description: The trail and surrounding property are located along the floodplain of the Des Plaines River. The Lake County Forest Preserve District purchased the property in the area with the intention of developing a 40-mile recreation corridor.

Although the trailhead may be reached from two areas from the north, probably the easiest place to begin the trail is at Van Patten Woods Forest Preserve. Van Patten Woods is located half a mile east of Route 41 off Route 173. Van Patten Woods divides the trail into two shorter sections: 6.3 miles to the south and 2 miles to the north.

A parking lot is available at Van Patten Woods. From the parking lot the rider may go to the picnic area and to Shelter A. From here a trail will be seen that goes

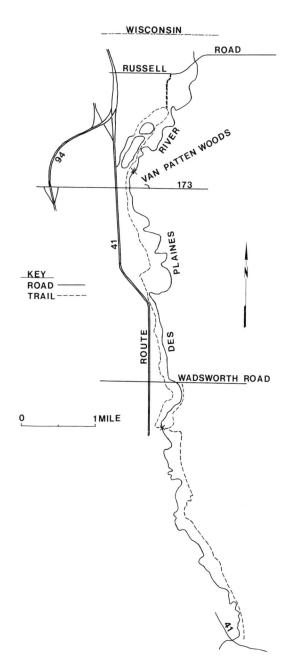

Des Plaines River Trail (Lake County), Northern Section

to a 200-foot bridge over the Des Plaines River. Once across the bridge, the rider may go north to the trailheads and Sterling Lake or south toward Route 173.

The trail north of 173 is 10–12 feet wide and is a dirt lane. This area all the way to the trailhead and around Sterling Lake may be extremely muddy during wet weather.

The section of trail south of Route 173 is surfaced with crushed stone and is generally about 12 feet wide. This portion of the trail is well maintained and is suitable for hiking, biking, horseback riding, cross-country skiing, and snowmobiling. The trail goes by open fields, prairie grass stands, and river floodplains. The trail also goes by some farm fields.

About one and a half miles south of Route 173 is a water pump that can be used for drinking water. The section of trail from the pump to Wadsworth Road is a prime viewing area for observing migratory birds such as long-neck geese.

South of Wadsworth Road the trail meanders through an area of importance—a new 450-acre Wetlands Demonstration Project. The Wetlands Project is a restoration of the Des Plaines River and marsh areas for flood control. The return of the marsh is expected to bring back waterfowl, fish, and other wildlife that thrive in a wetlands environment. The restoration project is most notable along the west side of the river.

South of Wadsworth Road, the trail passes through more dense woodlands than those of the northern part of the trail. The southernmost portion of the trail can be divided into two sections: one is U-shaped around the Des Plaines River from the west side of the river at Wadsworth Road, south to a 90-foot bridge, crossing over the river, then back north along the east side of the river, and ending at the Wadsworth Canoe Launch–Des Plaines River Trail Access.

The second southern section of trail begins at a trail junction on the east side of the bridge crossing over the river. This section meanders south paralleling the active railroad tracks and the river through dense woodland and marsh areas.

Periodically, there are green and white trail markers indicating the path is a multiuse section allowing snowmobiling.

From the trail junction on the east side of the bridge, the trail goes 2 miles south to a point about 500 feet short of Route 41. The southern end of the trail is effectively just beyond where a new bridge has been placed for further access to the trail along the Des Plaines River and marshlands. A wide variety of flora and fauna is visible along this section. The Des Plaines River Trail is expected to cross over Route 41 and continue south along the Des Plaines River, but funding for construction is not available at this time.

To return to the northern sections of trail, you must retrace your steps since this is not a loop trail.

Facilities: Water pumps, pit toilets, and car parking are located at the trailhead, at Van Patten Woods Forest Preserve, and at Wadsworth Canoe Launch. A canoe launch, fishing dock, observation platform, car and trailer parking, drinking water, and pit toilets are available at the Wadsworth Canoe Launch area. Van Patten Woods also has picnic grounds, shelters and playgrounds, additional trails, first-aid stations, and public telephones. Fishing is allowed in the Des Plaines River and Sterling Lake with all Illinois fishing rules and regulations in effect.

Trail Rules and Regulations: No hunting, swimming, fires, or littering. Pets must be on a leash. No amplified music allowed. Parking in designated areas only. No consumption of alcoholic beverages in or within immediate vicinity of parking areas.

Hours Open: 8:00 A.M. to sunset

Mailing Address and Phone Number: Lake County Forest Preserves, 2000 North Milwaukee Avenue, Libertyville, IL 60048; 847-367-6640

7. North Shore Bike Path

Trail Length: 12.2 miles, one way

Trail Surface: Crushed rock, short section of asphalt, and short section of concrete sidewalk

County: Lake

Location: The North Shore Bike Path is located in northeastern Illinois. The path goes through the communities of North Chicago, Waukegan, Beach Park, Zion, and Winthrop Harbor.

Access and parking are at Greenbelt Forest Preserve, Dugdale Road Parking Lot. To reach Greenbelt Forest Preserve go east on Belvidere Road (Route 120) eight-tenths of a mile to Green Bay Road. Follow Green Bay Road south to Tenth Street and go east to Dugdale Road. At Dugdale Road go south to the parking area entrance on the west side of Dugdale Road. The North Shore Bike Path can be reached by traveling northeast on Dugdale Road to the trail (eight-tenths of a mile) or take Dugdale Road to Tenth and go east about half a mile to the path. Other parking may be found along side streets throughout the communities the path passes through.

Trail Description: The North Shore Bike Path is a crushed limestone path (for 8.3 miles of the total length), built on or along the former North Shore Railroad. The crushed limestone path ends at the intersection of Twentieth Street, Broadway, Commonwealth Avenue, and Glenn Drive at Boak Park in North Chicago. There is an extension of the North Shore Trail south of Boak Park; following Commonwealth Avenue south, the path is asphalt and concrete marked with a yellow stripe. At Twenty-fourth Street the path goes east under Route 137 to Sheridan Road. After crossing to the

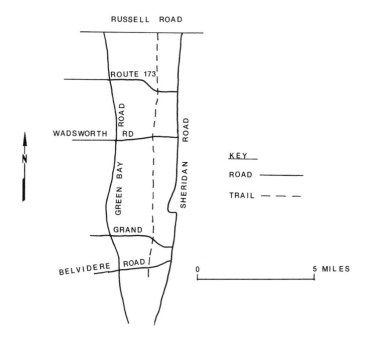

RUSSELL ROAD

ROUTE 173

WADSWORTH RD

ROAD

GREEN BAY

SHERIDAN ROAD

GRAND

BELVIDERE ROAD

KEY

ROAD ——————

TRAIL — — —

0   5 MILES

North Shore Bike Path. Redrawn from Illinois Department of
Transportation County Highway map.

west side of Sheridan Road, the North Shore Bike Path becomes sidewalk as it heads south. At D Street across from the Great Lakes Naval Training Center, the North Shore Bike Path officially ends, but the bike path is now asphalt paved and joins the Green Bay Trail going south toward Lake Bluff.

The main section of the path goes north from Boak Park, in North Chicago, all the way to the Illinois-Wisconsin border.

A secondary access point is located at Lyons Woods, which is on Blanchard Road, west of Sheridan Road between Sunset Avenue and Yorkhouse Road. There is a parking lot available and easy access to the North Shore Bike Path. For trail riders who want to divide the trail into shorter segments, Lyons Woods in Waukegan is about midpoint and is very convenient.

The path is well marked at street crossings and along the path with a large round metal marker and posts indicating direction and the name of the trail.

Riding north from North Chicago, the path passes through Waukegan and Beach Park, crossing several streets. Most of the path passes through residential neighborhoods and parks. Occasionally, there are some small wooded areas and open fields and remnants of the prairie that once existed throughout the area.

In Waukegan, there is a nature preserve along the North Shore Bike Path, Larsen Nature Preserve, Waukegan Park District.

Between Carmel Boulevard and Bethlehem Avenue in Zion Township, the path is recognized as a Zion Park District trail, but is a continuation of the North Shore Bike Path. This 1.5-mile section is asphalt paved.

From Bethlehem Avenue north, the path goes 2.3 miles through open fields as it reaches the bridge overpass at Russell Road, which is the Illinois-Wisconsin Border.

In Wisconsin, the path continues north and is called the Kenosha County Bicycle Trail.

Facilities: There are no established facilities on the trail, but numerous restaurants, bicycle shops, and other services are available in each community.

Park Rules and Regulations: Obey all Illinois Bicycle Rules of the Road.

Hours Open: Sunrise to sunset (unofficial)

Mailing Address and Phone Number: Lake County Division of Transportation, 600 West Winchester Road, Libertyville, IL 60048; 847-362-3950

8. McDonald Forest Preserve

Trail Length: 3.25 miles

Trail Surface: Crushed rock

County: Lake

Location: McDonald Forest Preserve is located in northern Illinois at the eastern border of Lindenhurst. The park entrance is on Grass Lake Road seven-tenths of a mile west of Route 45.

Trail Description: The trail system at McDonald Forest Preserve is a combination of two loop trails. The longer loop trail is 2.25 miles, meanders around a pond and through prairie restoration, and borders some wooded areas. This trail also has some steep hills making a challenging up and down hill ride. At about two-thirds of a mile from the parking lot, along the west side of the main loop, is the trail junction for a wood chip trail. This trail loop is 1 mile long and is narrower than the crushed rock trail. The wood chip trail is more hilly and borders a residential area and dense woods. The wood chip trail intersects the main trail south of a bridge crossing the pond.

Facilities: Parking, water, and latrines are available at the Grass Lake Road entrance.

Park Rules and Regulations: Park only in designated areas. Leash and pick up after all pets. Swimming, hunting, collecting, firearms, and off-road vehicles are prohibited. State fishing regulations apply.

Hours Open: 8:00 A.M. to sunset

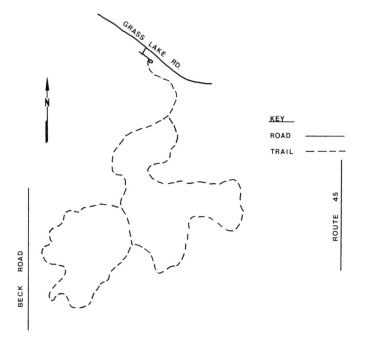

McDonald Forest Preserve. Redrawn from forest preserve map.

Mailing Address and Phone Number: Lake County Forest Preserves, 2000 North Milwaukee Avenue, Libertyville, IL 60048; 847-367-6640

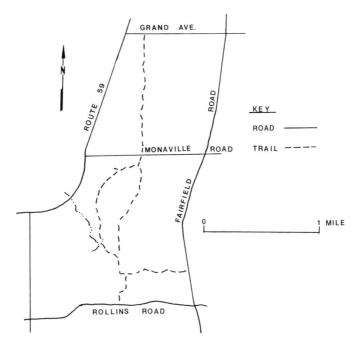

Grant Woods Forest Preserve

9. Grant Woods Forest Preserve

Trail Length: 4.5 miles

Trail Surface: Crushed rock

County: Lake

Location: Grant Woods Forest Preserve is located in northern Illinois near the southeast part of Fox Lake. Parking lots are available on Grand Avenue (Route 132) and Monaville Road, just east of Route 59.

Trail Description: The Grant Woods Trail System is multiuse for biking, hiking, and snowmobiling. The most popular section is accessed from the parking lot on Monaville Road.

South of Monaville Road the trail loops around a marsh area and passes through open fields of prairie restoration. At the southern end of the loop, the trail heads south and ends at Rollins Road. Another trail spur heads east to Fairfield Road (this spur is a trail junction midway between Rollins Road and the southern end of the loop trail). The total distance south of Monaville Road is 3.5 miles (one way).

The newest section of the Grant Woods trail begins or ends east of the parking lot at Monaville Road and goes north across Monaville Road. This section of the trail goes north 1 mile to Grand Avenue (Route 132). Most of this trail section meanders through open fields and prairie. During times of high water this section of the trail may be closed to prevent erosion.

Facilities: Parking, latrines, and drinking water are available at the Monaville Road and Grand Avenue entrances.

Park Rules and Regulations: Park only in designated areas. Leash and pick up after all pets. Swimming, hunting, collecting, firearms, and off-road vehicles are prohibited. State fishing regulations apply.

Hours Open: 8:00 A.M. to sunset

Mailing Address and Phone Number: Lake County Forest Preserves, 2000 North Milwaukee Avenue, Libertyville, IL 60048; 847-367-6640

10. Des Plaines River Trail (Lake County), Southern Section

Trail Length: 8.75 miles, one way

Trail Surface: Crushed limestone, dirt

County: Lake

Location: The Des Plaines River Trail, Southern Section, in Lake County is located about 2 miles west of I-94 between Route 176 and Route 22. A convenient parking area, allowing the rider to divide the trail into shorter sections, is at the canoe launch area on Route 60 on the west side of the river just east of Milwaukee Avenue (Route 21).

Trail Description: The Southern Section of the Lake County Des Plaines River Trail is a multiuse trail for hiking, biking, horseback riding, running, and cross-country skiing.

The trail offers natural diversity of wooded areas, open prairies, river valley, and flood plains. This area is a natural corridor for wildlife, including migrating birds.

North of Route 60 the trail parallels the highway east through the woods and then curves north and parallels St. Mary's Road. This section of the trail passes through MacArthur Woods Dedicated Nature Preserve, where some open space is found. At St. Mary's Road the trail goes through a tunnel under the road and then passes near a residential area and parallels an active railroad.

At Old School Road the trail enters the Old School Forest Preserve. Old School Forest Preserve has a connecting trail along the southwest boundary that joins the Des Plaines River Trail and creates a 3-mile loop;

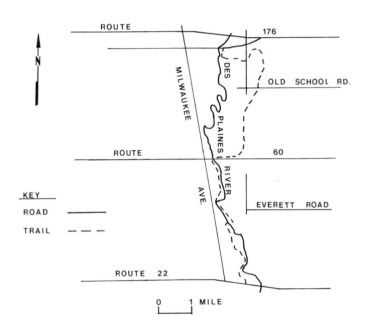

Des Plaines River Trail (Lake County), Southern Section. Redrawn from forest preserve map.

this connecting trail is found at the south side of the entrance to Old School Forest Preserve on St. Mary's Road. The remaining section of the trail crosses St. Mary's Road at the forest preserve, meandering east and north to the trail end at Old Rockland Road.

Between St. Mary's Road and Old Rockland Road there is mostly open meadows and restored prairie offering a great view of the Des Plaines River Valley.

At Route 60, the trail passes under the road. From Route 60 bending south to Route 22 (Half Day Road) the trail is much closer to the river bank and open prairie restoration as well as wooded areas. The trail goes on the west side of the river here. As the rider approaches Wright Woods the trail crosses the river via a large bridge.

The Des Plaines River Trail connects to the northwesternmost loop trail from the Wright Woods Trails (see trail 11) and then goes west by a bridge over the river and meanders southeast, as it passes through the Half Day Preserve section of the trail.

Half Day Preserve is a well-established forest preserve area offering restrooms, water, parking, picnic area, fishing access, shelters, and camping. From here the trail again passes through open fields and wooded areas as it heads toward the southern end at Half Day Road (Route 22).

Facilities: There are no facilities available immediately along the trail, but emergency services are at Old School Forest Preserve, Wright Woods, and at Half Day Forest Preserve. Parking is available at these forest preserve areas and at the canoe launch on Route 60, east of Milwaukee Road.

Telephone, water, restrooms, picnic areas, and fishing are available at Old School Forest Preserve, Wright Woods, and Half Day Forest Preserve.

Park Rules and Regulations: No loitering or picnicking within 100 feet of the parking lots, unless indicated. Illinois fishing regulations apply. No boating or swimming at forest preserve lakes. Carry out your own garbage, and do not disturb others or wildlife.

Hours Open: 8:00 A.M. to sunset

Mailing Address and Phone Number: Lake County Forest Preserves, 2000 Milwaukee Avenue, Libertyville, IL 60048; 847-367-6640

11. Wright Woods Forest Preserve

Trail Length: 4.75 miles

Trail Surface: Crushed rock

County: Lake

Location: The entrance to Wright Woods Forest Preserve is at the intersection of St. Mary's Road and Everett Road near Lincolnshire.

From I-94 exit at Half Day Road (Route 22), go west eight-tenths of a mile to Riverwoods Road. At Riverwoods Road go north about 1.6 miles to Everett Road. Go west on Everett Road 1 mile to St. Mary's Road and the entrance to Wright Woods Forest Preserve.

Trail Description: Wright Woods trails are a series of loop trails, all connecting, allowing for shorter or longer distances. The trails at Wright Woods are multiuse for biking, hiking, skiing, and horseback riding.

The trail on the west side of the parking lot is also the shortest trail, going around the lake, approximately one-half mile. The second longest loop trail is at the northwest area of the lake and lake trail and heads west and south, where it meets with the Des Plaines River Trail southern section and bridge, crossing over to Half Day Forest Preserve. This loop trail is approximately six-tenths of a mile. A longer loop trail leaves the parking area, past the ranger station, and heads northwest and then connects to the Des Plaines River Trail (Lake County), southern section. Follow this trail south from the trail junction 1.5 miles to a trail junction that goes north, back to the parking lot. This loop trail is about 2 miles in all.

The eastern part of Wright Woods has two larger

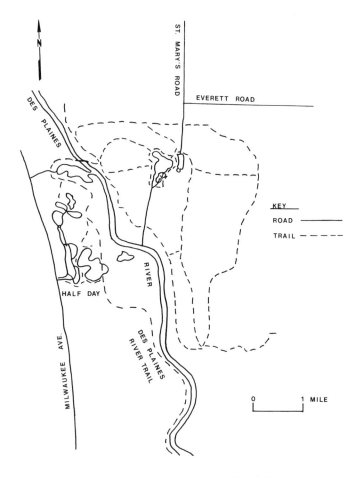

Wright Woods Forest Preserve. Redrawn from forest preserve map.

loop trails and a smaller one as well as a spur trail leading to an open prairie.

From the northeast corner of the parking lot take the trail south about 1/8 mile to a trail junction, go east 1/4 mile to the next trail junction, and go north 3/4 mile to the next trail junction and go south back to the parking lot. This loop trail is about 1.25 miles and passes through mostly densely wooded area.

The largest loop trail leaves the northeast corner of the parking lot and goes south 1 mile to a four-way trail junction; the immediate northeast trail heads north 1.25 miles, via a connecting trail, west back to the parking area. The trail east is the spur trail meandering out to the open prairie. This trail is not a loop trail and therefore has to be used for return (about 1/3 mile one way).

There is a shorter loop trail on the southwest side of Wright Woods that parallels the river and connects with another loop trail and eventually connects with the Des Plaines River Trail once again.

The trail system at Wright Woods is well maintained. The entire forest preserve is noted for its sugar maples and various native plantings.

Facilities: Picnic areas, playground, water, restrooms, shelters, telephone, and emergency services are at the ranger station. Hiking, biking, skiing, and horseback riding.

Park Rules and Regulations: Park only in lots. Leash and pick up after pets; swimming, hunting, collecting, firearms, and off-road vehicles are prohibited. State fishing regulations apply. Permits are required for horseback riding, picnics, shelters, and gatherings of 25 or more people.

Hours Open: 8:00 A.M. to sunset, daily

Mailing Address and Phone Number: Lake County Forest Preserves, 2000 North Milwaukee Avenue, Libertyville, IL 60048; 847-367-6640

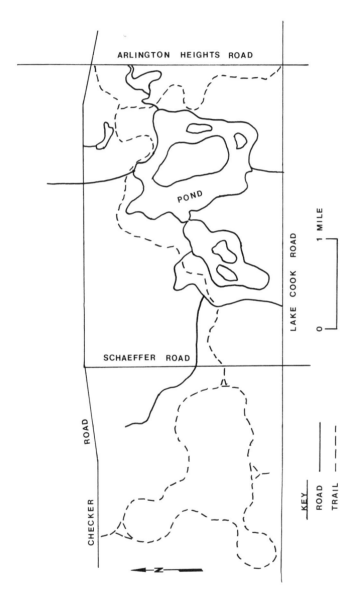

Buffalo Creek Forest Preserve. Redrawn from forest preserve map.

12. Buffalo Creek Forest Preserve

Trail Length: 4.25 miles

Trail Surface: Crushed rock

County: Lake

Location: The preserve and trail are located at the corner of Checker Road and Arlington Heights Road, near Buffalo Grove.

The main east-west road for access is Lake-Cook Road, which is the southern boundary of the preserve. Buffalo Creek Forest Preserve is about 3 miles west of Milwaukee Avenue (Route 21) and about 3 miles east of Rand Road (Route 12).

Trail Description: The trail system in Buffalo Creek Forest Preserve is accessed at the parking lot and entrance on Checker Road, just west of Arlington Heights Road. The majority of the trail meanders west, across Schaeffer Road, where the trail becomes a 2-and-a-half-mile loop trail. There is a trailboard and marker at the start of the loop, just west of Schaeffer Road.

Most of the loop trail is in open prairie and tall grass allowing the rider to see the majority of the acreage at any point of the trail. The preserves are surrounded by residential areas.

The trail crosses several creeks, borders a reservoir-lake, and passes through restored prairie land. This area is designed and managed for flood control, resulting in a natural-looking wetland area.

The newest trail section is a one-way spur that leaves the main trail at the parking area and heads southeast to Arlington Heights Road. It passes the dam as it parallels Arlington Heights Road and the eastern boundary of the preserves.

Facilities: Fishing, parking, and drinking water.

Park Rules and Regulations: Park only in designated areas. Leash and pick up after all pets. Swimming, hunting, collecting, firearms, and off-road vehicles are prohibited. State fishing regulations apply.

Hours Open: 8:00 A.M. to sunset

Mailing Address and Phone Number: Lake County Forest Preserves, 2000 North Milwaukee Avenue, Libertyville, IL 60048; 847-367-6640

13. The Great Western Trail (Du Page County)

Trail Length: 12 miles, one way

Trail Surface: Limestone screenings

County: Du Page

Location: The Great Western Trail is a linear trail that goes through central Du Page County, including the municipalities of Villa Park, Lombard, Warrenville, and Carol Stream. To reach the eastern trailhead, travelers can take Route 83 to Roosevelt Road. Follow Roosevelt Road west one mile to Villa Avenue. Turn south on Villa Avenue and go to Central Avenue. Found here is the parking lot for the Villa Park Historical Society Museum and the Illinois Prairie Path; the Great Western Trail is located 2 blocks north of the museum.

Trail Description: The Great Western Trail–Du Page County, is a 12-mile rail-trail along the former Chicago and Great Western Railroad. The trail goes through numerous communities and parks and is multipurpose for bicyclists, hikers, cross-country skiers, and horseback riders. The western terminus of the trail connects with the Illinois Prairie Path, Elgin Branch (trail 19).

Starting north of the museum, the trail can go west or east. Heading east, the trail only goes for a short distance to Route 83. There is little use in this trail section and better trail riding is found along the Illinois Prairie Path, which is parallel to this section.

The Great Western Trail is marked with brown signs. Stop signs are also found along the numerous roads that have to be crossed. The trail is about 6 to 8 feet wide and has a limestone screened surface. The trail at the eastern end starts out by going through residen-

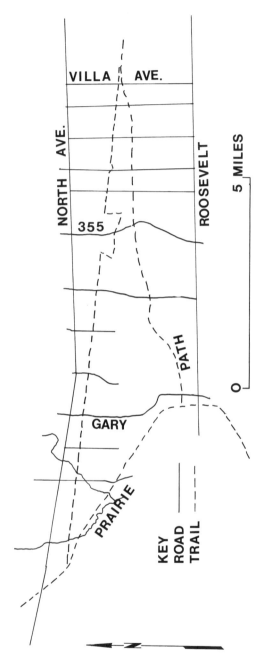

The Great Western Trail (Du Page County). Redrawn from Du Page County Transportation map.

The Great Western Trail

tial and commercial properties and as you head farther west you go through more rural areas.

In 1996, there were two main detours found along the trail. The first detour was at Highland Drive. A barricade prevents you from going on here. On the left you will see St. Charles Place. Follow St. Charles Place west to Grace Avenue. Go over the railroad tracks and on the left will be the trail again, where you will see a sign for the Great Western Trail.

This next segment goes by some beautiful residential properties. In addition there are some nice wildflowers seen growing along the trail. Some of the residential streets that dead-end into the trail have connecting paths to the trail.

The second detour is located at West Street. If you continued ahead, you would pass under a bridge and then be stopped at I-355. A new overpass bridge is being built to get over I-355. Until it is completed, follow West Street south to St. Charles Road. St. Charles Road is a busy street. Head west on St. Charles Road, go over I-355, past Churchill Woods Forest Preserve (see Trail 17), to Swift Road. Turn right on Swift Road and at the top of the hill near the substation you will see the trail continuing.

Past the substation is a wetland area and farther on are some soccer fields. Some major roads have to be crossed and there are some additional developments. Cross over a wooden bridge at Klein Creek. Across a second small bridge is Timber Ridge Forest Preserve. Near here are a pond and a small marsh. Shortly past this pond the Great Western Trail meets the Illinois Prairie Path.

Currently, the trail junction is not marked and the trails are not level. You must take some stairs down to reach the Prairie Path. In the future the Du Page County Division of Transportation expects to improve this junction.

The rider then can continue on the Illinois Prairie Path and make a nice loop ride by taking the Elgin Branch to the Main Stem and heading east on the Main Stem all the way back to the Villa Grove Historical Museum.

Facilities: The Villa Grove Historical Society Museum has some restrooms; refreshments are available. Numerous communities found along the trail also have places to stop. A few parks along the trail including Timber Ridge Forest Preserve and Churchill Woods Forest Preserve also have restrooms and water.

Park Rules and Regulations: Motorized vehicles are prohibited. Pets must be leashed at all times.

Hours Open: Open year round

Mailing Address and Phone Number: Division of Transportation, Du Page County, 130 N. County Farm Road, P. O. Box 298, Wheaton, IL 60189-0298; 630-682-7318

14. Virgil L. Gilman Nature Trail

Trail Length: 11 miles, one way

Trail Surface: Crushed limestone, asphalt

County: Kane

Location: The Virgil L. Gilman Nature Trail is located in northeastern Illinois, beginning south of Aurora in the town of Montgomery. From Chicago and the east, the trailhead is reached via Illinois Tollway I-88. Exit the tollway at Route 31 south and follow 31 south through Aurora into Montgomery to Montgomery Road.

Go 1.3 miles east on Montgomery Road to Ohio Street (some maps show this as Hill Avenue) and turn south for .7 mile to the trailhead. The trailhead is on the west side of Ohio Street and has a small parking area and trail information board. The trail can also be reached from Bliss Woods Forest Preserve, on Bliss Road about half a mile east of Route 47 (north of Route 56 and south of Waubonsee Community College).

Trail Description: The Virgil L. Gilman Nature Trail follows the railroad right-of-way of the Elgin, Joliet, and Eastern Railroad, and the Chicago, Milwaukee, St. Paul, and Pacific Railroad. Most of the trail is a smooth, crushed-limestone path about 6 feet wide; some sections are asphalt.

Most of the path is easy to follow from any access point; however, one section in Aurora is somewhat difficult. Between Terry Avenue and Lake Street (Route 31), the trail actually becomes the sidewalks winding through this residential and industrial neighborhood. There are signs (white arrows on a brown background) indicating travel direction for the path, but only a few are scattered along this six-block section.

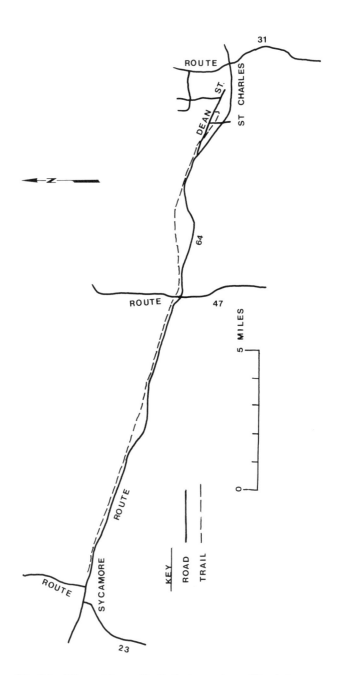

Virgil L. Gilman Nature Trail. Redrawn from Illinois Department of Transportation Highway map.

Traveling east, the path at Terry Avenue goes one quarter block north to the first intersection then east to Elmwood Drive. Go north on Elmwood Drive for one block, then east for one block. At the stop sign, turn south one block to the parking lot where the trail is located. The opposite directions are appropriate for going westbound.

The trail passes through rural, suburban, and urban areas. Some sections offer a view of farmlands; others pass through residential areas as well as some commercial-industrial areas. One section near Waubansee Creek has a marsh adjacent to the trail.

Native plants and wildlife of Illinois can be seen along most sections of the trail. Some of the trees that can be seen include cottonwoods, white poplars, sycamores, and oak. Birds seen along the trail include duck, heron, redwing blackbirds, woodpeckers, cardinals, and bluejays.

Probably the most interesting section of the trail is west of Terry Avenue, where the trail passes through its most densely wooded section. Another interesting section is the crossing of the truss bridge spanning the Fox River.

At the west end the trail crosses Galena Boulevard and continues half a mile to Route 56, where one can cross over Route 56 or follow the safer alternative of using the tunnel. West of Route 56 the trail parallels Blackberry Creek as it meanders 2 more miles across Bliss Road to Bliss Woods Forest Preserve. This section of trail offers good views of native plants and wildlife, as well as of rural and residential areas.

The newest section of trail parallels Route 25, heading south to Mill Street. A future extension will take the trail down to Yorkville.

Facilities: Numerous parking and access points are available for the Virgil L. Gilman Nature Trail at the Bliss Woods Forest Preserve, at Galena Boulevard east of Gordon Road, Barnes Road near the Blackberry Historical Village, Orchard Road, Jericho Road at Edgelawn Drive (Copley No. 1 Park) Route 31, Route 25, Ashland Avenue, Montgomery Road, and Ohio Street.

Restrooms and shelters are available at Lebanon Park on Douglas Avenue, at Copley No. 1 Park, along the trail just east of Orchard Road, and at Bliss Woods Forest Preserve. Picnic areas are also available at several of the access points and parking areas in Aurora, at the Galena Boulevard parking area and at Bliss Woods Forest Preserve. Limited camping is available at Bliss Woods Forest Preserve.

Trail Rules and Regulations: No camping, fires, dumping, or littering, and no hunting.

Hours Open: Sunrise to sunset

Mailing Addresses and Phone Numbers: Fox Valley Park District, 712 South River Street, Aurora, IL 60506; 630-897-0516; Kane County Forest Preserve District, 719 Batavia Avenue, Geneva, IL 60134; 630-232-1242

15. Pratt's Wayne Woods Forest Preserve

Trail Length: 10 miles

Trail Surface: Dirt, grass, limestone screenings

County: Du Page

Location: Pratt's Wayne Woods State Park is located near Wayne, in the northwest corner of Du Page County near Kane County. To reach the park, travelers may take Route 59 to Army Trail Road. Turn west on Army Trail Road and go 2 miles to Powis Road. Turn north on Powis Road and head one mile to the park entrance, marked by a sign on the left side of the road.

Trail Description: Pratt's Wayne Woods consists of more than 2,600 acres of open area, wetlands, prairies, and woods. There are a few trail access points throughout the park, and the trail system is found on both the west and east sides of the park.

If you use the main park entrance, you may park at either the first or second parking area to get on the trail. If you park at the first parking area, you can ride your bike back to the park entrance to get on the trail and then head north. The trail goes through a small wooded area, by the second parking area, and behind the youth campground.

A connecting trail south takes the rider back toward the ponds, or one can continue west toward an open field. The trail heads south back toward the ponds and then a connecting grass trail heads west through the open field toward the horse jumping area. You will go by a horse training and competition area.

The trail heads into the woods where you take a fork in the trail left; the trail comes out to the Illinois Prairie Path. On the Prairie Path, there is no sign for the Pratt's Wayne Woods Forest Preserve, so you may not

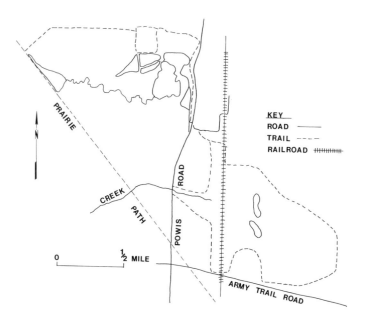

KEY
ROAD
TRAIL
RAILROAD

PRAIRIE

CREEK PATH

POWIS ROAD

0   ½ MILE

ARMY TRAIL ROAD

Pratt's Wayne Woods Forest Preserve. Redrawn from forest preserve map.

find the park easily. You then head southeast on the Prairie Path going by a few wetlands, wooded areas, over Norton Creek, and then the trail comes out at Powis Road.

You travel north on Powis Road for about a quarter mile, and the trail is found on the east side of the road on the north and south sides of Norton Creek. If you go in on the trail on the south side of the creek, the trail heads southeast through a large open field. It comes to the Commonwealth Edison right-of-way lines and heads south to Army Trail Road.

The trail crosses the EJ&E Railroad track and then makes its way through another field. This loop area seems to be used by horse riders. The trail does a big half loop through this open field and goes by a small pond and a dog training field. The rider must then cross the EJ&E Railroad tracks again and go through an open field back toward Powis Road. A connecting trail takes the rider back behind the maintenance facility and along the north side of Norton Creek.

You cross the road then and are back at the main park entrance.

Facilities: Picnic facilities, water, restrooms, youth campgrounds, shelters, and fishing ponds are available here.

Park Rules and Regulations: Ride only on multipurpose trails. Stay on the right-hand side of the trail except when passing on the left from behind. Ride single file, especially when passing on the left. Always ride under control and watch your speed and trail conditions, especially around curves. No motorized vehicles, all-terrain vehicles, or motorcycles on the trails. No swimming in the ponds. No bicycling on the trails around the ponds.

Hours Open: The park is open 1 hour before sunrise and closed 1 hour after sunset.

Mailing Address and Phone Number: Forest Preserve District of Du Page County, 185 Spring Avenue, Glen Ellyn, IL 60138; 630-790-4900

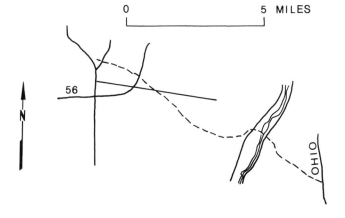

The Great Western Trail. Redrawn from Illinois Department of Transportation map.

16. The Great Western Trail

Trail Length: 17 miles, one way

Trail Surface: Limestone screenings

Counties: De Kalb and Kane

Location: The Great Western Trail is located in northeastern Illinois 2 miles west of St. Charles. The east trailhead is located on the south side of Dean Street opposite the entrance for LeRoy Oakes Forest Preserve. On Route 64, both east and west, signs for LeRoy Oakes Forest Preserve can be seen. From Route 64 follow Randall Road north to Dean Street. Go west on Dean Street for half a mile and turn south, across from the entrance for LeRoy Oakes Forest Preserve.

The west trailhead is located in Sycamore at the intersection of Route 64, Old State Road, and Airport Road. Sycamore is located at the intersection of Route 23 and Route 64, 5 miles north of De Kalb.

Trail Description: The Great Western Trail is a crushed-stone path about 10 feet wide. It parallels the north side of Route 64 for 17 miles. Previously, the trail was a railroad bed, and evidence of the old railroad ties and markers can still be seen.

The right-of-way of the Great Western Trail was developed into a railroad in 1887 by the Minnesota and Northwestern Railroad. Later that same year the Chicago, St. Paul, and Kansas Railway purchased all property of the Minnesota and Northwestern Railroad. At its peak, the Chicago Great Western operated 1500 miles of track connecting Illinois, Iowa, Kansas, Minnesota, Missouri, and Nebraska.

Along the 17-mile path are several prairie sites, marshes, wetlands resembling bogs, and several small, densely wooded areas. The trail also passes along several active farms and through the small communities of Wasco, Lily Lake, Virgil, Richardson, and Sycamore.

At several points along the trail, adjoining woodlands have been developed into subdivisions. Mile markers are located on either side of the trail; these markers are wooden posts about 1 foot high, with red numbers on them, and they are located a foot or two off the crushed-stone path. The trail also has stop signs at all road crossings, and there is a stop signal at Burlington Road, a hazardous crossing.

Wildlife in the area includes deer, raccoon, opossum, beaver, fox, skunk, rabbit, and woodchucks. Also, a great variety of birds can be seen, including ducks, coot, and the great blue heron.

Primary users of the trail are bicyclists, mostly because of the trail length and because there are no camping facilities along the trail. The trail is also popular for cross-country skiers. LeRoy Oakes Forest Preserve and the Sycamore Community Park are the only established parking areas on the trail.

The Great Western Trail is a National Recreation Trail. A future trail extension is proposed from LeRoy Oakes Forest Preserve to hook up to the Fox River trail system. A 6-mile trail extension is slated for construction between Sycamore and De Kalb in 1997.

Facilities: Restrooms are available at the trailhead (LeRoy Oakes Forest Preserve), at the Wasco crossing, and at Sycamore Community Park. Water is available at LeRoy Oakes Forest Preserve, Wasco, Virgil, and Sycamore Community Park.

Picnic tables and two shelters are located along the trail. Picnic tables are located between LeRoy Oakes and Wasco, 1 mile west of Route 47, just west of County Line Road, and at both trailheads. Shelters are available at Virgil, Lily Lake, and the trailhead opposite LeRoy Oakes Forest Preserve.

Trail Rules and Regulations: No horseback riding and no motorized vehicles. Hunting is not allowed, and pets must be on a leash.

Hours Open: The preserve is open from 8:00 A.M. to 9:00 P.M. Monday through Friday and from 7:00 A.M. to 9:00 P.M. Saturdays and Sundays. Trail users are urged to complete their journey by sundown.

Mailing Address and Phone Number: Kane County Forest Preserve District, 719 Batavia Avenue, Geneva, IL 60134; 630-232-1242

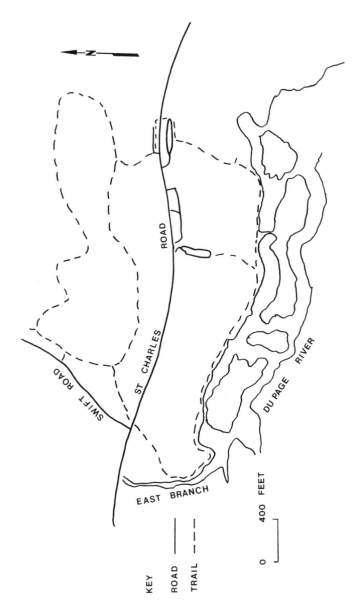

Churchill Woods Forest Preserve. Redrawn from forest preserve map.

KEY

ROAD

TRAIL

17. Churchill Woods Forest Preserve

Trail Length: 3.5 miles

Trail Surface: Dirt, grass

County: Du Page

Location: Churchill Woods Forest Preserve borders I-355 to the east in Glen Ellyn. To reach the park, travelers can take I-355 to the North Avenue exit. Head west on North Avenue for 2 blocks and turn south on Swift Road. Take Swift Road 1 mile to St. Charles Road and turn east. The park's two entrances will be on the south side of the road.

Trail Description: The trail at Churchill Woods Forest Preserve consists of two short trails on the north and south sides of Swift Road. The trail starts at one of the parking areas found on the south side of Swift Road. Trailboards are seen at these parking areas.

The trail goes down toward the Du Page River, where it heads west, paralleling the river for a short distance and passing by a youth camping area. It then heads into the woods and north toward Swift Road, where the biker must cross the road, which is busy at times.

The trail continues on the north side of the road. There is a loop trail that goes through a small wooded area, around a large prairie and a small wetland. During the rainy season, the trail at the northeast end may be under water. The trail then goes up a small hill at the northeast corner and comes out at Swift Road and a frontage road. Follow the frontage road east where you will go under the road. The trail then comes out to a second parking area where there is a trailboard.

Follow the trail south to the river and then back toward the first parking area. A causeway also takes the

Churchill Woods Forest Preserve

Trailboard, Churchill Woods Forest Preserve

biker between some ponds. Lots of geese are seen here and many people fish the ponds and river.

Facilities: Water, restrooms, youth camping area, and picnic tables are found here.

Park Rules and Regulations: Ride only on multipurpose trails. Stay on the right-hand side of the trail except when passing on the left from behind. Ride single file, especially when passing on the left. Always ride under control and watch your speed and trail conditions, especially around curves. Alcoholic beverages are prohibited.

Hours Open: The park opens one hour after sunrise and closes one hour after sunset.

Mailing Address and Phone Number: Forest Preserve District of Du Page County, 185 Spring Avenue, Glen Ellyn, IL 60138; 630-790-4900

Churchill Woods Forest Preserve

Typical trail markers, Churchill Woods Forest Preserve

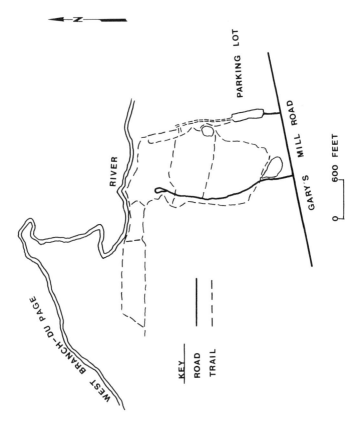

West Du Page Woods Forest Preserve. Redrawn from park
trail map.

18. West Du Page Woods Forest Preserve

Trail Length: 4 miles

Trail Surface: Dirt, grass

County: Du Page

Location: West Du Page Woods is located in Winfield. One mile west of the intersection of Roosevelt Road (Route 38) and Winfield Road is Gary's Mill Road. Turn east onto Gary's Mill Road and go about five blocks to the parking area. This is the Elsen's Hill area. To reach the west part of the park, take Route 59. Three quarters of a mile north of Roosevelt Road is the park entrance on the east side of Route 59.

Trail Description: West Du Page Woods was acquired in 1919 and is one of the oldest of the Forest Preserve District of Du Page County's 43 preserves. It has 470 acres of upland woods and one of the few fens in Du Page County.

West Du Page Woods offers two areas to ride. The first is at the Elsen's Hill area on Gary's Mill Road. The second location is at the west entrance off Route 59.

The trail system at the Elsen's Hill area consists of four interconnecting loops that total 4 miles. The trail system may be started north of the parking area by a small pond. An information board showing a trail map is set up at the north end of the parking lot.

Here the trails are marked with brown fiberglass posts that have different symbols on them such as circles, which identify the loops. These trails may be ridden in any direction and are also used by hikers, horseback riders, and cross-country skiers.

Most of the trails go through upland forest, passing residential homes on the west side of the park and paralleling the west branch of the Du Page River on the north. The trail also goes by a small pond and around Elsen's Hill.

Future plans call for having the Regional Trail extend from Blackwell Forest Preserve (see trail 20) through here and then hook up with a spur of the Illinois Prairie Path (trail 19).

The trail at the west end of West Du Page Woods, off Route 59, consists of a 2-mile loop.

Facilities: West Du Page Woods has an information board, water, restrooms, picnic tables, and a site superintendent's home.

Park Rules and Regulations: Ride only on multipurpose trails. Stay on the right-hand side of the trail except when passing on the left. Always ride under control and watch your speed and trail conditions, especially around curves. Pets must be on a leash. Alcoholic beverages are prohibited.

Hours Open: The preserve is open every day of the year, from one hour after sunrise to one hour after sunset.

Mailing Address and Phone Number: Forest Preserve District of Du Page County, 185 Spring Avenue, Glen Ellyn, IL 60138; 630-790-4900

19. The Illinois Prairie Path

Trail Length: 55 miles

Trail Surface: Limestone screenings

Counties: Kane, Du Page, Cook

Location: The Illinois Prairie Path is located in north-eastern Illinois. It has five main branches from Wheaton: one branch goes northwest to Elgin; the second goes past the West Chicago Prairie to the Fox River and auxiliary trails; the third goes southwest to the East-West Tollway I-88 and then west and northwest to the Fox River and Batavia; the fourth goes southwest, as does the third branch, but then goes farther southwest of the East-West Tollway to Aurora; and the fifth branch goes east to Maywood.

The great length and number of main branch trails make access and distance planning very easy. The trail goes through many communities, including Maywood, Bellwood, Berkeley, Elmhurst, Villa Park, Lombard, Glen Ellyn, Warrenville, Aurora, Winfield, Batavia, Geneva, West Chicago, South Elgin, and Elgin. All the main branches of the Illinois Prairie Path join at Carlton Avenue and Liberty Street in Wheaton. The midpoint is Elmer J. Hoffman Park in Wheaton, which is on Prospect Road (north-south), off Hill Avenue, just one-half block east of where Hill Avenue crosses the railroad tracks. See Facilities for other trail access points and parking locations.

Trail Description: The Illinois Prairie Path is a multi-purpose trail available for biking, hiking, cross-country skiing, and horseback riding. It follows the route of the former Chicago, Aurora, and Elgin Railway. The Illinois Prairie Path, a not-for-profit corporation, was the idea of Mrs. May Theilgoord Watts, distinguished natu-

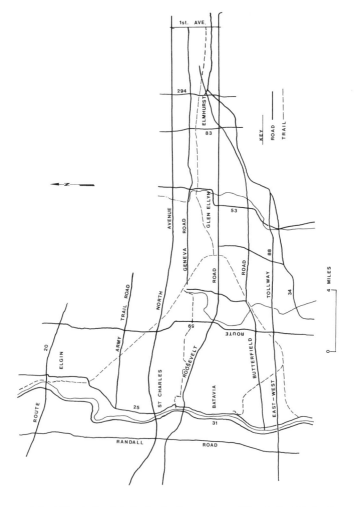

The Illinois Prairie Path. Redrawn from Illinois Prairie Path-map.

Trailboard, The Illinois Prairie Path

ralist, teacher, and author. Local response and the cooperation of utility companies and civic leaders along with state, county, and municipal officials played a vital role in the path's development.

In 1966, the path was formally established under a lease granted by Du Page County, owner of the rights-of-way. On June 2, 1971, a major portion of the path was designated a Recreation Trail of the National Trails System, becoming the first trail in Illinois to be so designated. The Illinois Department of Conservation purchased the Kane County segments of the rights-of-way in 1972 and leased the property to the Forest Preserve District for use as part of the path. In 1979, the state acquired 4.5 miles of right-of-way in Cook County to First Avenue in Maywood.

From the historic bridge over the Chicago and Northwestern Railway in Wheaton, the branch to Elgin passes through wooded areas, such as the Lincoln Marsh (1 mile from the bridge), the Timber Ridge Preserve, and Pratt's Wayne Woods Forest Preserve. This segment also connects with the Great Western Trail, Du Page County (see trail 13). The Lincoln Marsh has a

Historic CA&E bridge, The Illinois Prairie Path

connecting trail to the short nature trail in the wetland ecosystem. Farther northwest, the trail passes through residential and rural communities, many times bordering farm fields. This section is generally about 6 feet wide and is composed of crushed limestone.

In Elgin, at Raymond Street and Purify Drive, the Prairie Path is linked to the Fox River Trail. Wooden posts with yellow numbers are the mile markers along the trail. Most crossings have the name of the road and show the Prairie Path emblem, a green oval with three railroad spikes forming an inverted Y. Also, within the oval are the symbols for footprints, a horseshoe, and a bicycle wheel. At Kenyon Road, where the Model Railroad Club is located, is the Clintonville Station of the Chicago, Aurora, and Elgin.

Bicyclists along The Illinois Prairie Path

The branch of the Prairie Path from Wheaton east to First Avenue in Maywood may be the most popular trail section, because it passes through many developed areas. From Wheaton going east, the path passes through Glen Ellyn, Lombard, Villa Park, Elmhurst, Berkeley, Bellwood, and Maywood. Many of the communities have taken advantage of the railroad rights-of-way by developing parks along the path. These parks often have benches and water available. Some points of interest along this branch of the Prairie Path include the Villa Avenue CA&E Station, the Elmer J. Hoffman Park in Wheaton, and Wheaton College.

The trail sections from Wheaton to Batavia and Aurora are similar in composition to the other branches, that is, crushed limestone. From the historic bridge in Wheaton the path runs parallel to Carlton Avenue two blocks south to Roosevelt Road. Just south of Roosevelt Road is the Prairie Path Park owned by the Wheaton Park District (another Prairie Path park is in Glen Ellyn).

The newest section of the Prairie Path (Geneva Spur, 9 miles) connects to the Fox River Trail at Bennett Park in Geneva. This trail segment was dedicated on

Bridge over creek, The Illinois Prairie Path

June 1, 1996, along with the Jack T. Knuepfer Bridge spanning the Union Pacific and Elgin, Joliet and Eastern Railroads. This bridge is located next to Reed-Keppler Park. Beginning at the intersection of County Farm Road and Geneva Road, in Winfield, go west along Geneva Road to Winfield Road. Head south on Winfield Road, where the trail turns into Winfield Mounds Forest Preserve, crosses a small bridge and snakes its way to the old railroad grade.

At Prince George Crossing in West Chicago, the trail is part of Main Street, making its way through residential areas and downtown and past the old railroad station. The trail then makes its way to Reed-Keppler Park and over the Jack T. Knuepfer Bridge. Not far beyond the bridge is the West Chicago Prairie. The trail will cross over a few roads, go through a tree-lined canopy, and go right next to the Du Page County Airport. Past the airport the trail continues to East Side Drive. Turn north at East Side Drive and follow to High Street. Take a left on High Street and go 2 blocks, until the trail continues in a wooded area.

Follow this trail, going by a cemetery until you

reach Route 25, where you come down a wood platform to cross the road. The trail then joins the Fox River Trail on the east side of the river.

Just north of East-West Tollway I-88 along Eola Road is another trail junction referred to as the Batavia Spur. This trail junction can make a convenient connecting trail for a shorter ride and loop trail; for example, riding from Aurora northeast to Batavia and then back south with the Fox River Trail can make a 15-mile loop section. To complete this loop, go northwest from Eola Road and the East-West Tollway to the Fox River in Batavia and cross over to the west side of the river via Wilson Road. Then follow the Fox River Trail south to Illinois Avenue in Aurora; go east to reach the Prairie Path again.

Facilities: Water fountains are located in various parks along the trail. Restaurants, gas stations, and other businesses are located in almost all the communities through which the path travels. For camping areas contact the Du Page and Kane County Forest Preserves listed below. Free parking is available at the following sites: in Elmhurst, east of York Road between Vallette Street and the path and west of Spring Road north of the path; in Villa Park, west of Villa Avenue on Central Boulevard; in Lombard, west of Westmore Avenue; in Glen Ellyn, Hill Avenue between Glen Ellyn and Lombard; in Wheaton, at the County Courthouse parking lot; near Elgin, at County Farm and Geneva Road; in Aurora, at McCullough Park, Illinois Avenue; and in Geneva, Bennett Park, at Route 25.

Park Rules and Regulations: No motorized vehicles, alcoholic beverages, or firearms. No kite or model airplane flying allowed. No camping or cookouts allowed.

Hours Open: The area is open year-round. No restricted hours, but daylight hours are standard for safety reasons.

Mailing Addresses and Phone Numbers: Illinois Prairie

Path, P.O. Box 1086, Wheaton, IL 60189; 630-752-0120; Forest Preserve District of Du Page County, 185 Spring Avenue, Glen Ellyn, IL 60137; 630-790-4900; or Kane County Forest Preserve District, 719 Batavia Avenue, Geneva, IL 60134; 630-232-1242

20. Blackwell Forest Preserve

Trail Length: 6.5 miles

Trail Surface: Dirt, limestone screenings

County: Du Page

Location: The Blackwell Forest Preserve borders Butterfield and Winfield Roads in Warrenville. The main entrance to South Blackwell Forest Preserve is off Butterfield Road (Route 56), west of Winfield Road. To reach the trailhead at North Blackwell, travelers may take Winfield Road to Mack Road. Turn west on Mack Road, go 1.2 miles, and turn into the parking lot on the north side of the road. From Route 59, turn east on Mack Road and go half a mile. A sign there identifies McKee Marsh parking. A trailboard and restrooms are located at this trailhead.

Trail Description: Early in 1960 the Forest Preserve District of Du Page County purchased a worked out gravel pit as part of their land reclamation program because of its excellent potential as a multiuse recreation area. The gravel pit was to be transformed into a large recreational lake and to serve as a major rainwater retention basin. In order for this plan to be realized, the gravel pit needed to be deeper and larger.

At the same time that the lakes were being excavated, the county leaders were concerned about the growing problem of solid waste disposal in Du Page County. The district developed a plan that would solve the problems of waste disposal and clay disposal from the construction of the lake.

A hill constructed of refuse was built next to the lake. Clay removed from the lake was used to cover the refuse. When the hill was completed, it was transformed into a winter sports area. This hill, now known as Mt.

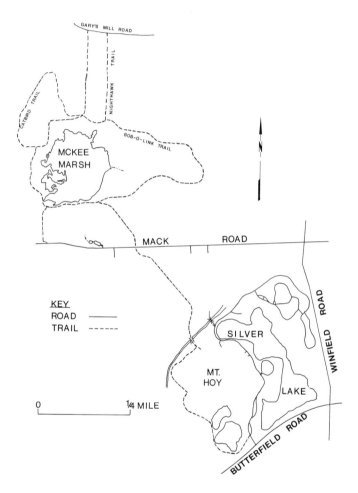

Blackwell Forest Preserve. Redrawn from park map.

Hoy, rises more than 150 feet above its surroundings, making it the highest point in Du Page County.

The district purchased adjacent forest and meadowland to increase the size of the preserve to more than 1,300 acres. The preserve is named in honor of a former board president, Roy C. Blackwell. Blackwell Preserve consists of two tracts: North Blackwell and South Blackwell. South Blackwell encompasses the recreation facilities, while North Blackwell remains virtually undeveloped.

The trail system at Blackwell Forest Preserve may be started or ended at North or South Blackwell areas. The main trail at South Blackwell is the Regional Trail (1.6 miles). This trailhead is found near the first parking spot off Butterfield Road. Directly across from the parking area, a sign identifying McKee Marsh parking will be seen.

The Regional Trail is an 8-foot-wide pebbled trail. The trail winds its way on the south side of a small pond. Mt. Hoy, the main landmark in South Blackwell, can be seen constantly by the rider. A hiking trail makes its way up the north side of Mt. Hoy. From here you have a good view of the park and the surrounding area. A tubing run is set up here for winter enthusiasts.

Once past Mt. Hoy, the trail goes into a wooded section and will shortly come to Springbrook Creek. Here the rider will cross over a small steel bridge and then ride through an open field. This trail segment heads northwest toward Mack Road. A trail sign will be seen near the road. The rider then crosses this road and continues at North Blackwell. The trails at North Blackwell consist of a large loop (Bob-o-Link Trail), a segment of the Regional Trail that terminates at Gary's Mill Road, an old road bed that also terminates at Gary's Mill Road (Nighthawk Trail), a small loop trail (Catbird Trail), and a short connecting trail that leads to the parking area and trailhead.

The Bob-o-link Trail is a 3-mile crushed rock and dirt loop around McKee Marsh. It goes through open fields and some low-lying areas where many bird species can be observed.

On the north side of McKee Marsh, the trail joins

the Regional Trail and the Nighthawk Trail, which the rider can take to Gary's Mill Road, or one can ride a little trail loop known as the Catbird Trail, which goes through a wooded area and near the west branch of the Du Page River. The west side of McKee Marsh is wooded and pretty, with some good views of the marsh.

Cross-country skiing is allowed on any of the multipurpose trails in the park.

Facilities: Blackwell Forest Preserve has campgrounds (60 units, open seasonally), a boat launch, a tubing run, and numerous picnic sites that have tables, restrooms, water, and shelters. Fishing is allowed in Silver Lake contingent upon all Illinois fishing rules and regulations.

Park Rules and Regulations: Ride only on multipurpose trails. Stay on the right-hand side of the trail except when passing on the left from behind. Ride single file, especially when passing on the left. Always ride under control and watch your speed and trail conditions, especially around curves. Pets must be on a leash. No boat shall be more than 20 feet in length. No gas motors, no inflatable crafts, rafts, or pontoons, and no wind-surfing are allowed.

Hours Open: The preserve opens one hour after sunrise and closes one hour after sunset every day of the year.

Mailing Address and Phone Number: Forest Preserve District of Du Page County, 185 Spring Avenue, Glen Ellyn, IL 60138; 630-790-4900

21. Fullersburg Woods Forest Preserve

Trail Length: 3.8 miles

Trail Surface: Dirt, rock, asphalt

County: Du Page

Location: Fullersburg Woods is located in Oak Brook, west of the Tri-State Tollway I-294 and north of Ogden Avenue (Route 34). From Ogden turn north on York Road. At the Y intersection of York Road and Spring Road go northwest onto Spring Road. Follow Spring Road about 1 mile to the park entrance, on the north side of the road.

Trail Description: The trails at Fullersburg Woods consist of two loop trails; the longer one meanders around the Visitor Center (2.5 miles), and a shorter loop (1.3 miles) goes north of there.

Both of these loop trails are multiuse trails for biking, hiking, and skiing. There are other trails located in Fullersburg Woods, but only the two loop trails mentioned are open for biking. All of the trails can be started at the Visitor Center.

Maps and a trailboard are found at the Visitor Center for easy trail identification, as well as information about the preserve.

The longer bike trail is an asphalt path from the park road, heading south, paralleling Salt Creek to the historic Graue Mill at York Road. At York Road go left and cross over the creek bridge to reach the trail northbound.

This section is a combination of dirt and crushed rock; it meanders along the higher bluff of Salt Creek and borders a residential area to the east. Eventually this trail loops west and south and connects with the Interpretive Trail.

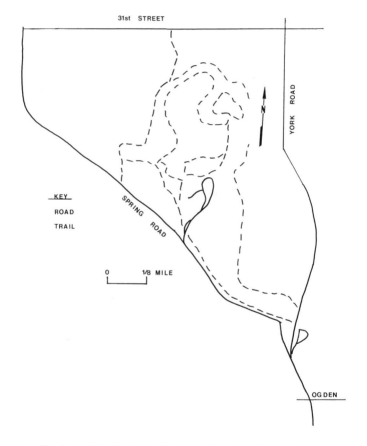

Fullersburg Woods Forest Preserve. Redrawn from forest preserve map.

The Interpretive Trail is a multipurpose hiking, biking, and skiing trail. It follows the lower part of the creek valley and also crosses over to a shorter loop via a bridge. Both loop trails offer a variety of scenery including open meadows, wetlands, open water areas, and woodlands. The trails are located in and throughout what is established as a nature sanctuary for plants and animals. There are nature education and information boards located along the trails describing various natural findings of the area.

Facilities: Graue Mill, at the south end of the trail on York Road, is a National Historic Landmark.

The Visitor Center is open daily from 9:00 A.M. to 5 P.M. except July 4th, Thanksgiving, Christmas Eve, Christmas Day, and New Year's Day.

Fullersburg Woods Environmental Education Center is also found here and has facilities and scheduled programs for environmental and nature topics. Latrines, telephone, water, and parking are available.

Park Rules and Regulations: No collecting allowed. Pets must be leashed. Other restrictions as posted.

Hours Open: Open daily, from an hour after sunrise until an hour after sunset

Mailing Address and Phone Number: Fullersburg Woods Forest Preserve, 3609 Spring Road, Oak Brook, IL 60521; 630-790-4900

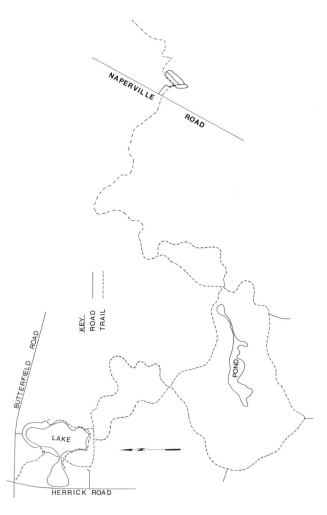

Herrick Lake Forest Preserve and Danada Forest Preserve

22. Herrick Lake Forest Preserve and Danada Forest Preserve

Trail Length: 8.5 miles

Trail Surface: Limestone screenings

County: Du Page

Location: Herrick Lake and Danada Forest Preserves are located in Wheaton. Both preserves may be reached by Butterfield Road (Route 56). Herrick Lake is 2 miles west of Naperville Road and one mile east of Winfield Road. The main entrance to the park is off Butterfield Road, with a second entrance to the park from Herrick Road. Herrick Road is located just west of the main entrance. Turn south on Herrick Road and proceed a few blocks to the parking area. To reach Danada Forest Preserve, take Butterfield Road to Naperville Road. Turn south on Naperville Road and proceed less than a mile to the park entrance, on the east side of Naperville Road.

Trail Description: Herrick Lake Forest Preserve consists of 764 acres of woodlands including a 22-acre natural lake that was formed when the Wisconsin Glacier retreated fourteen thousand years ago. Danada Forest Preserve is home to the Danada Equestrian Center.

The trail system at Herrick Lake consists of three loops that total 6.5 miles, with a connecting spur (Regional Trail) to Danada Forest Preserve. This trail system is multipurpose; hikers, bicyclists, and horseback riders use it. The trailhead at Herrick Lake may be reached from the parking lots off Butterfield Road or Herrick Road. There is an information board set up at both parking lots showing the trail layout. A trailboard is found at the north end of the parking lot at Danada Forest Preserve.

Rider along the regional trail, Danada Forest Preserve

From the parking lot off Butterfield Road, a biker can pick up the trail on either side of Herrick Lake. The entire trail is surfaced with limestone screenings. The trail on the west side of the lake connects with another spur trail to Herrick Road. A short distance north of Herrick Road is the Illinois Prairie Path.

Following the Herrick Lake trail around the lake, the rider will go past the other parking area and a shelter. The trail then hooks up with the main trail and the three loops.

The first loop segment, Meadowlake Trail, takes the rider through some wooded areas and past the golf course. Meadowlark Trail is about 10 feet wide and leveled with limestone. The trail then joins the second loop in the middle of an open field.

Riders can then choose which direction to go. To the west, Green Heron Trail goes through some pretty wooded sections and prairies. Trail spurs connect to Herrick Road and Warrenville Road. To the east is a small wooded area and a small prairie and beyond that a small pond. Shortly past the pond is the third loop segment, Bluebird Trail, which goes around a small grassy area and borders recreation facilities on the east side. It is here that a trail connects to Danada Forest Preserve and its 2 miles of trails.

The trail segment to Danada Forest Preserve goes though a large open field with beautiful views of a prairie and wetlands. A trailboard is seen along the trail, and the trail heads east past the equestrian center, through a tunnel under Naperville Road, and to the parking area. The trail continues for a short distance past this parking area.

Riders can then follow the trail system back to the trailhead at Herrick Lake.

Facilities: Herrick Lake Forest Preserve has picnic areas with shelters, picnic tables, restrooms, and water available. On the northern shore of the lake, a concessionaire sells snacks and rents rowboats and canoes. A youth camping area is also available in the preserve. Fishing is allowed in Herrick Lake with all appropriate rules and regulations in effect.

Found at Danada Forest Preserve are an equestrian facility, water, restrooms, and a small lake.

Park Rules and Regulations: Ride only on multipurpose trails. Stay on the right-hand side of the trail except when passing on the left from behind. Ride single file, especially when passing on the left. Always ride under control and watch your speed and trail conditions, especially around curves. Pets must be on a leash. Alcoholic beverages are prohibited. Private boating is prohibited, and motorized vehicles are prohibited on the grounds.

Hours Open: The preserve is open every day of the year, one hour after sunrise until one hour after sunset.

Mailing Address and Phone Number: Forest Preserve District of Du Page County, 185 Spring Avenue, Glen Ellyn, IL 60138; 630-790-4900

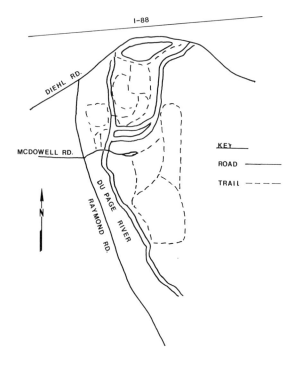

McDowell Grove Forest Preserve. Redrawn from park map.

23. McDowell Grove Forest Preserve

Trail Length: 3 miles

Trail Surface: Dirt, grass, limestone screenings

County: Du Page

Location: McDowell Grove Forest Preserve is found in western Du Page County, south of I-88 and east of Route 59. To reach the park travelers on I-88 can exit south on Route 59. Turn east on McDowell Road and head to Raymond Road. Directly ahead at Raymond Road is McDowell Grove Forest Preserve, where the main parking area is found. There is a single-lane bridge over the west branch of the Du Page River when you first enter the preserve.

Trail Description: The trail system at McDowell Grove Forest Preserve consists of a series of small loop trails that wind their way around the preserve on the north and south sides of the west branch of the Du Page River. To reach the trails at the north end of the preserve, ride across the bridge over the west branch and get on the trail near the road.

This part of the trail system goes through some nice wooded areas, crosses a tributary of the west branch and goes through some wooded uplands. A few loops in here make it fun, and then the trail system heads north toward Mud Lake. The trail stays on the south side of Mud Lake, with trail spurs going on the west and east sides of the lake. Part of the trail at Mud Lake consists of limestone screenings. The trail heads south along the west branch of the Du Page River, goes back to the small tributary crossing and then back toward the park entrance.

The trail on the south side of the Du Page River is a large loop with connecting spurs that starts near the

Entrance sign, McDowell Grove Forest Preserve

trailboard. It goes through a small wooded area, paralleling the river, and then by an open field and a beautiful residential area. The trail continues south past these homes on a wide grassy surface, runs into a connecting trail, and soon heads west back toward the river. Heading north, parallel to the river, the trail goes to the rightand goes back toward the open field or continues to the parking area.

Facilities: Water, restrooms, picnic area, and a shelter are found here, and fishing is allowed in the Du Page River.

Park Rules and Regulations: Alcoholic beverages are prohibited. Fishing from the bridge is prohibited. Never ride on trails or roads posted closed to bicyclists. Watch for trail conditions. Bicyclists are prohibited on trails less than 8 feet wide. No more than two bicyclists abreast, and stay on right side of trail.

Hours Open: The park opens 1 hour after sunrise and closes 1 hour after sunset.

Mailing Address and Phone Number: Forest Preserve District of Du Page County, 185 Spring Avenue, Glen Ellyn, IL 60138; 630-790-4900

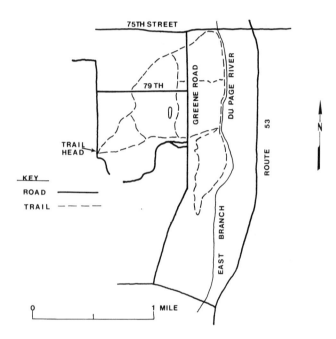

75TH STREET

79 TH

GREENE ROAD

DU PAGE RIVER

TRAIL
HEAD

ROUTE 53

N

KEY

ROAD

TRAIL

EAST BRANCH

0   1 MILE

Greene Valley Forest Preserve

24. Greene Valley Forest Preserve

Trail Length: 7 miles

Trail Surface: Grass, dirt

County: Du Page

Location: Greene Valley Forest Preserve is located 3 miles west of Woodridge. To reach the park, take Route 53 to Seventy-fifth Street and turn west. Go five blocks to Greene Road, turn south onto Greene Road, and go to Seventy-ninth Street. Turn west on Seventy-ninth Street and go a few blocks to the west access area of the forest preserve. Turn south on this road and proceed to the trailhead.

Trail Description: Greene Valley Forest Preserve is named after the Greene family, who settled and farmed the area. The site consists of 1,441 acres. Greene Valley Forest Preserve's trail system consists of interconnecting loop segments that total more than 7 miles in length. The trail system is multipurpose, with biking, hiking, skiing, and horseback riding allowed. An information board is found at the parking lot in the west access area. The information board provides a trail map and park rules.

The trails may be ridden in any direction and on any of the loops. There are a few cutbacks along the trails that can reduce the number of miles ridden. Geometric symbols on brown fiberglass posts mark the trails. The trail system consists of a mowed grass path about 12 feet wide.

The main trail is designated with a white circle and starts at the trailhead. One segment of the main trail heads due east and goes by the site superintendent's home. This part of the trail goes through open fields. The trail comes to one of the cutback trails, which goes north. The trail heading north goes by three small ponds, through woodlands, open fields, along power lines, and over Seventy-ninth Street twice.

Trails on the east side of Greene Road parallel the east branch of the Du Page River and join with one of the cutbacks. The southern loop trail segment goes through an open field, with landfill to the west. The trail also goes through some woods and then heads back north to the main trail segment, which the rider can follow back to the trailhead.

Facilities: Greene Valley Forest Preserve has an information board, restrooms, drinking water, telephone, and seventeen campsites set up for youth camping only. There is a designated area for dog sledding.

Park Rules and Regulations: Ride only on multipurpose trails. Stay on the right-hand side of the trail except when passing on the left from behind. Ride single file, especially when passing on the left. Always ride under control and watch your speed and trail conditions, especially around curves. Pets must be on a leash. No trespassing around the landfill site. Alcoholic beverages are prohibited.

Hours Open: The preserve is open every day of the year 1 hour after sunrise until 1 hour after sunset.

Mailing Address and Phone Number: Forest Preserve District of Du Page County, 185 Spring Avenue, Glen Ellyn, IL 60138; 630-790-4900

25. Waterfall Glen Forest Preserve

Trail Length: 8.5 miles, loop

Trail Surface: Dirt, grass, gravel

County: Du Page

Location: Waterfall Glen Forest Preserve is located in northeastern Illinois approximately 25 miles southwest of Chicago. The most direct route to the parking area and trailhead is via I-55 to Cass Avenue South. About one-eighth mile south of I-55 is the entrance to the frontage road where the parking area and information building can be seen. Just beyond the information building, on Northgate Road, turn west to the main parking area and trailhead.

Waterfall Glen Forest Preserve surrounds Argonne National Laboratory, which is centered between north-south Route 53 and Route 83, just south of I-55.

Trail Description: The trail system at Waterfall Glen Forest Preserve surrounds Argonne National Laboratory. This area is a glacial till deposited by the Wisconsin Glacier.

At the trailhead an information board with a map displays the trails and identifies the other facilities available at Waterfall Glen.

The trail system is designed as a multipurpose trail and is used by bikers as well as hikers, horseback riders, cross-country skiers, and those interested in orienteering.

The trail system at Waterfall Glen consists of a main trail that circles Argonne National Laboratory and is 8.5 miles long. Connected to the main trail are three loop trails known as Tearthumb Swamp Cutback, Westgate Road Cutback, and the Kettle Hole Woods

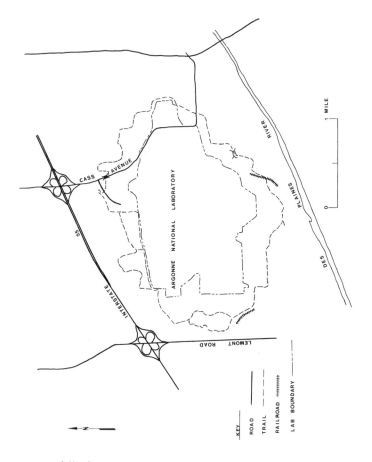

Waterfall Glen Forest Preserve.

Bridge over creek, Waterfall Glen Forest Preserve

Cutback. By taking one of these loops, the biker can shorten the length of the ride.

Brown fiberglass trail markers have a geometric symbol corresponding to the trail. The main trail is designated by a white circle. Most of the trails are wide grassy lanes, except for the main trail between the campground and Kettle Hole Woods Cutback, which is a combination of crushed stone paths and gravel roads. All three loop segments pass through tall stands of evergreens, occasionally along bogs, and in several locations right through or right next to marsh. One side of the loop segment of the Tearthumb Swamp Cutback and Westgate Road Cutback follows along the fence surrounding Argonne Laboratory. The main trail, which passes along marshes, bogs, and prairies, and through densely wooded areas, offers more variety than the shorter loop segments. A great variety of wildlife may be observed along the marshes of the main trail. A model airplane field is also located along this path.

On a high ridge at the southernmost point of the main trail is a scenic area overlooking the Des Plaines River Valley. An information board is found here. Another scenic view may be had from the iron footbridge.

Trailboard, Waterfall Glen Forest Preserve

Here the trail crosses over Sawmill Creek (there is a ford for horses) and offers a fine view of the V-shaped valley. A third attraction, probably the highlight of this trail, is the small waterfall located half a mile west of the outdoor education camp.

All along this trail system are footpaths, roads, and other wide lanes that intersect the main trail. The rider must stay on the established trail. At Waterfall Glen there is a variety of wildlife. The animals most frequently seen are the native whitetail deer and the white fallow deer imported from Asia. Many migratory birds can be seen here.

Facilities: Restrooms, parking, and drinking water are available at the trailhead and outdoor education camp. Orienteering courses are established along the northeast corner of Waterfall Glen.

Park Rules and Regulations: Ride only on multipurpose trails. Stay on the right-hand side of the trail except when passing on the left from behind. Ride single file, especially when passing on the left. Always ride under control and watch your speed and trail conditions, especially around curves. Never ride on trails or roadways posted as closed to bicyclists. No alcohol is allowed on preserve grounds. No collecting or hunting of trees, shrubs, flowers, or wildlife, except mushrooms, is permitted.

Fires must be contained in fireplaces and grills provided, or in a burner. Cutting and gathering firewood is not permitted. Pets are allowed, but must be on a leash at all times.

Hours Open: One hour after sunrise to one hour after sunset

Mailing Address and Phone Number: Forest Preserve District of Du Page County, 185 Spring Avenue, Glen Ellyn, IL 60138; 630-790-4900

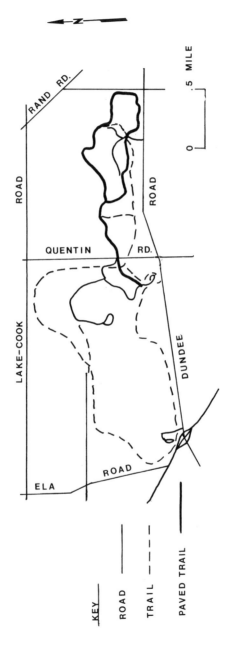

Deer Grove Forest Preserve. Redrawn from park trail map.

26. Deer Grove Forest Preserve

Trail Length: 5+ miles

Trail Surface: Dirt, limestone screenings

County: Cook

Location: Deer Grove Forest Preserve is located in Palatine, off Dundee Road. To reach this preserve, take Route 53 to Dundee Road. Turn west on Dundee Road and proceed 3 miles to the Deer Grove East parking lot. Parking is also available at Deer Grove West by taking Dundee Road to Quentin Road. Turn north on Quentin Road and proceed for a quarter of a mile to the entrance of Deer Grove West, located on the west side of the road. Bikers can also park at Camp Reinberg, which is on the east side of Quentin Road, opposite the entrance for Deer Grove West.

Trail Description: The Deer Grove Forest Preserve Mountain Bike Trail is shared by horseback riders and cross-country skiers. It winds its way through Deer Grove West and East Tracks; Quentin Road divides the park. The main loop trail is in Deer Grove West, while a short piece is in Deer Grove East. The trail is predominantly dirt, with a small segment in limestone screenings.

In 1996 this trail system was officially opened to mountain bikers after an agreement was reached with forest preserve officials. Prior to this, erosion and damage was being caused by off-trail usage. Mountain biking is now limited to the designated trail, which is marked with gray trail markers. Those trails that are off-limits to mountain bikers and horseback riders are marked.

The mountain bikers' trail begins at the northern part of the first parking area in Deer Grove East. The trail is composed of limestone screenings at this location. The trail segment heading northeast currently terminates at the paved bike path. The segment heading southwest makes its way into the woods and then comes by the paved bike path, which it parallels for a short distance. Where the paved bike path goes north, the mountain bikers' trail heads into the woods. There a short segment to the right takes the mountain biker to the paved bike path again. The trail then goes by an old water treatment plant and some buildings—all part of Camp Reinberg. The trail heads left and crosses Quentin Road to reach Deer Grove West.

The trail system at Deer Grove West is an excellent area for mountain bike riding. A long loop trail segment is found at this location, and some good riding and beautiful wooded areas are found. The trail goes over the paved bike path a few times as well as over the park road. Many other trails are found in this area but they are off limits to mountain bike riders. There are two trailboards at the parking areas. At the north end of the loop, there is a small connecting trail segment that goes to Hillside Road. A few small creeks are also crossed as well as a few bridges. The trail is predominantly level, with a few small hills.

At the east end of this loop, the trail goes over the park road as well as the paved bike trail, connecting up with the original trail, which takes you back to Deer Grove East.

Facilities: Deer Grove Forest Preserve has various parking areas, restrooms, a few small ponds, and water.

Park Rules and Regulations: Motorized vehicles are prohibited on trails. Bicyclists and equestrians must stay on the designated trail. No off-trail riding is allowed. Be courteous to other trail users. Bicyclists yield to hikers and equestrians. Give notice before passing other trail users. Do not ride on unpaved trails when the trail is muddy. Recreational use only. No speed training (8 m.p.h. maximum speed). All trails are two-way. Stay in your lane. Don't litter.

Hours Open: The forest preserve closes at sunset.

Mailing Address and Phone Number: Forest Preserve District of Cook County, 536 North Harlem Avenue, River Forest, IL 60305; 708-771-1330

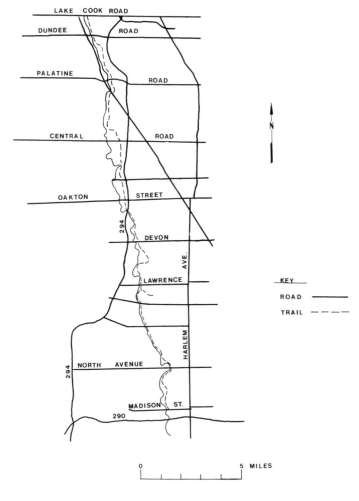

Des Plaines River Trail (Cook County). Redrawn from Illinois Department of Transportation Cook County Highway map.

27. Des Plaines River Trail (Cook County)

Trail Length: 27 miles

Trail Surface: Dirt, gravel

County: Cook

Location: The Des Plaines River Trail is located in northeastern Illinois along the eastern bank of the Des Plaines River. From Madison Street in Forest Park, the trail passes through many suburbs of Chicago north to Lake-Cook Road, which is the border between Lake County and Cook. Major access points include the Potawatomi Woods and Dam No. 1 Woods off Dundee Road; Allison Woods and the River Trail Nature Center off Milwaukee Avenue at Winkelman Road; Camp Pine Woods off Euclid Avenue; Big Bend Lake off East River Road; and Golf Road in Des Plaines. All of the afore-mentioned areas are considered part of the Des Plaines Division of the Forest Preserve District of Cook County.

Major access points between Touhy Avenue in Park Ridge and Madison Street in Forest Park include Axe-head Lake off Touhy Avenue; Dam No. 4 east off Dee Road or Devon Avenue; Robinson Woods south off Lawrence Avenue; Schiller Woods north off East River Road–Montrose Avenue or Irving Park Road in Schiller Park; Evans Field off Thatcher Avenue; and Thatcher Woods and Thatcher Woods Glen off Chicago Avenue in River Forest. All of these areas are considered part of the Indian Boundary Division of the Forest Preserve District of Cook County.

Trail Description: The Des Plaines River Trail passes through the narrow band of native landscape along the eastern bank of the Des Plaines River in Cook County.

The area is rich with the history of the many Indians who once lived here.

Evans Field is the site of an Indian village; east of Evans Field, five mounds were built by prehistoric Indians. The Indian Boundary Line, which crosses the trail just east of Grand Avenue in River Grove, is the north line of a strip of land 20 miles wide from Lake Michigan to Ottawa ceded to the settlers by the Potawatomi Indians in 1816. Big Bend Lake is the site of an old Indian village, and Camp Pine Woods is the site of a pioneer cabin.

The Des Plaines River Trail in Cook County is the longest of three trails established along the Des Plaines River that are part of a proposal to make a linear recreational greenway from the trailhead at Sterling Lake, south of Russell Road in Lake County, to this trail in Cook County (trail 6).

The majority of the trail is a gravel and dirt path. Native trees and wildflowers are seen all along the trail. There are many species of birds visible in this area, including many migratory birds. Many deer and rabbit can be seen at different times of the year since the Des Plaines River and surrounding preserve are an excellent refuge for a variety of wildlife.

The Des Plaines River Trail is part of two different divisions of ten divisions in Cook County. The Cook County Forest Preserve District has some 150 miles of multipurpose trails available for bikers, hikers, horseback riders, and cross-country skiers. The two divisions of this trail are the Indian Boundary Division, from Touhy Avenue in Park Ridge to Madison Street in Forest Park, and the Des Plaines Division, from Touhy Avenue north to the Lake-Cook County border.

The Des Plaines River Trail is marked only by symbols of horses attached to posts at major road crossings (white figure on a brown background). The north end of the trail ends at Lake-Cook Road, which is a four-lane road. The south end stops at Madison Street. You will see a cemetery and cannot continue south of Madison Street.

Horses are allowed on this multipurpose trail, but the majority of horseback riders are seen between Golf

Road and Lake-Cook Road. One section of the trail that is a bit confusing is at the Allison Woods section. From the east, finish the gravel path at Allison Woods parking area and follow the entrance to Milwaukee Avenue. Cross Milwaukee Avenue and follow Winkelman Road beside the Holiday Inn for an eighth of a mile. The trail then goes west. Opposite directions are appropriate if you are traveling from west to east.

Another confusing section of the trail is between Rand Road and the crossing at Algonquin Road. Going north, cross Algonquin Road, go north on Campground Road past the Banner Day-Care Center and then the Methodist Camp. Continuing on Joseph Schwab Road, you will pass the Northwestern Woods.

Follow the Joseph Schwab Road under the viaduct to Northwest Highway. Turn east, and follow the sidewalk crossing the Busse Highway intersection, and then continue for two blocks to Garland Place. Turn north onto Garland Place and go one block to Rand Road. The trail is very visible directly across Rand Road. Be cautious when crossing Rand Road because it is hazardous.

South of Lawrence Avenue the trail becomes narrower, almost a footpath in parts, and is much closer to the bank of the river. In fact, much of the trail between Lawrence Avenue and North Avenue is the floodplain of the Des Plaines River. During wet seasons these sections may be impassable; one section that is difficult almost year round is between Grand Avenue and Belmont. This section is very low and is often flooded. A good alternate route is to go west from either Grand or Belmont Avenue to Des Plaines River Road. Then go north or south to your desired intersection, east again over the river, and continue the trail.

From the north crossing Belmont Avenue, the trail is hard to locate. Crossing Belmont, you will notice a cemetery. Continue south behind the guardrail and follow the iron fence toward the river. Upon reaching the last fencepost follow the narrow path around it and continue the trail south along the fence and cemetery property.

Another difficult section is near Fullerton Woods

East. The main trail goes east, while the connecting trail goes along the river, past a dam and a bridge, finally crossing the river. Follow the main trail to the east for about a quarter of a mile where another trail junction is reached. Again, follow the left trail, and you will find yourself at the water pump at Evans Field.

If you missed the turnoff for the main trail and do not desire to cross over the river (the trail would then end at First Avenue), there is a trail on the east side of the river at the foot of the bridge. This trail meanders through some floodplains and meets with the main trail to form the aforementioned junction. Follow the right trail, and again you will find yourself at the water pump at Evans Field.

From Evans Field follow the entrance out to Thatcher Avenue and continue south on Thatcher Avenue. Cross North Avenue and continue south about 100 yards where a section of guardrail is separated (about 4 feet wide). A new shelter should be visible just yards behind the guardrail. The trail continues past the shelter and along the river.

The remainder of the trail is but a footpath that passes through some densely wooded areas. At Chicago Avenue the trail becomes an asphalt path for a short distance past a lagoon and behind the Trailside Museum.

The Trailside Museum is an excellent place to stop and view a variety of birds and mammals native to this area. Many varieties of the wildlife on display are reestablishing themselves at this wildlife shelter; staff members are available for assistance.

South of the Trailside Museum, the trail divides into two sections that meet again and form a loop. The shorter route follows Thatcher Avenue south again just beyond the Chicago and Northwestern Railroad, where it turns into the woods and goes west. The longer route goes west through the woods, follows the bank of the river beyond the railroad tracks, and then moves east again to where the trails meet and form a loop beside a trail shelter.

Facilities: There are many trail shelters located along

this trail. Contact the Forest Preserve to find the exact locations of those available for use.

Water and restrooms are available at most of the forest preserve lands that have picnic areas; also, shelters and parking areas may be found at these forest preserves. A youth group campground is available at Camp Baden Powell on Des Plaines River Road south of the headquarters on Foundry Road in Mount Prospect.

Park Rules and Regulations: Use receptacles for garbage and trash. Report any fires. No alcoholic beverages allowed.

Hours Open: For safety reasons, use the trail during daylight hours only. The Forest Preserve District picnic grounds and parking areas close at sunset.

Mailing Address and Phone Numbers: For additional facilities maps and maps of the ten divisions of forest preserve districts in Cook County contact: Forest Preserve General Headquarters, 536 North Harlem Avenue, River Forest, IL 60305; 708-771-1330; Des Plaines Division Headquarters, River Road at Foundry Road, Mount Prospect, IL 60056; 847-824-1900 or 824-1883

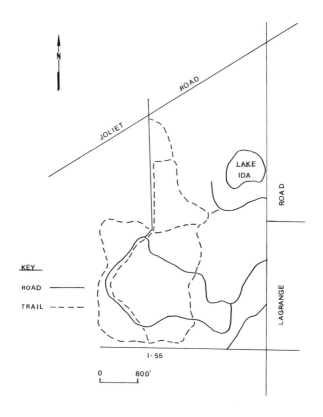

Arie Crown Forest Bicycle Trail. Redrawn from forest preserve map.

28. Arie Crown Forest Bicycle Trail

Trail Length: 3.2 miles

Trail Surface: Dirt, grass, rock

County: Cook

Location: Arie Crown Forest Preserve is located along LaGrange Road in Hodkins. To reach the preserve, take LaGrange Road (Route 45), from either the north or the south. The preserve borders Joliet Road on the north and I-55 on the south. There are two preserve entrances off LaGrange Road. The trailhead begins at Sundown Picnic Area, which is located north of 67th Street.

Trail Description: The trailhead for the Arie Crown Bicycle Trail is found at the last parking area in Sundown Meadow. A trailboard with the trail layout is found here. The trail heads into a wooded area and goes north where there will be a Y in the trail. If you turn right, you head toward Joliet Road. The trail is about 8 feet wide and mostly dirt.

A trail junction left takes the rider toward Brainard Road past an open field and apartment complexes and over a wooden bridge. A trail junction will be seen where the rider can cross the road and follow the trail on the southwest part of the park. Here the trail goes by some homes, and I-55 is on the south side. The trail is a little overgrown on this segment.

A trail junction just beyond the homes will take the rider to a trail that parallels the park road, and another trailboard is seen. The main trail on the east side of the park crosses the road two more times, goes up and down a few small hills and over two more small bridges. Soon there is a connecting trail that heads west or a trail that heads back to the trailhead.

The trail is a short and easy one to bike on, with a few loops in there to make the ride longer by looping around on the trails.

Facilities: There are restrooms, water pumps, and picnic tables, as well as a small lake.

Park Rules and Regulations: Motorized vehicles, wading, swimming, and boating are prohibited. Use only designated trails. Cyclists yield to all other trail users. All users should exercise caution, reduce speed when passing, and make their presence known to other trail users. Do not litter, and never disturb animals or trample plants.

Hours Open: Sunrise to sunset

Mailing Address and Phone Number: Forest Preserve District of Cook County, 536 North Harlem Avenue, River Forest, IL 60305; 708-771-1330

29. Palos and Sag Valley Forest Preserves

Trail Length: 36 miles

Trail Surface: Dirt

County: Cook

Location: The 14,000-acre Palos and Sag Valley Forest Preserves are located southwest of Chicago, directly west of Hickory Hills and Palos Hills.

The area is bordered on the west by Route 83, on the north by the Des Plaines River and Archer Avenue, on the east by Kean Avenue, and on the south by 135th Street and the Cook-Will County boundary. Route 45, LaGrange Road, and 96th Avenue are main roads north-south through the preserves.

Trail Description: The Palos Forest Preserve trails total 17.75 miles as established trails approved for biking, and are multiuse trails.

A convenient parking area to divide the trail system is at the Little Red School House Nature Center South of 95th Street, on 104th Avenue. West of 104th Avenue the trail system is mostly one way with spur trails leading to various road access points.

As the trail meanders west from 104th Avenue it passes through Pulaski Woods and Wolf Road Woods parking lots.

Most of the trail passes through densely wooded areas and nearby marsh areas known as sloughs. West of Wolf Road Woods and Tomahawk Slough the trail makes a short loop from which a spur trail heads northeast to Bullfrog Lake parking area. Another spur trail goes west to Archer Avenue, just south of the entrance to Red Gate Woods. Another spur trail heads southwest to Archer Avenue and ends about half a mile north of Route 83. This spur trail is less traveled.

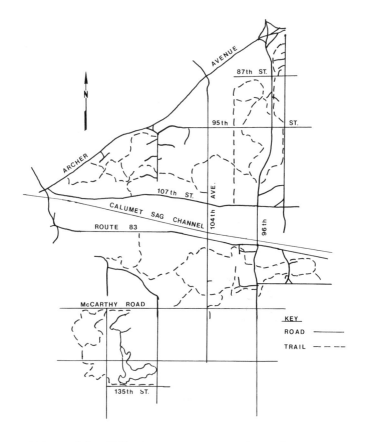

Palos and Sag Valley Forest Preserves. Redrawn from forest
preserve map.

Bike riders, Palos Forest Preserve

A fourth spur trail, from the loop, heads south to Saganashkee Slough parking area at 107th Street. East of 104th Avenue, the trail is a combination of longer loop trails. These loop trail segments are between 104th Avenue and Kean Avenue.

The trail is well maintained and easy to follow.

North of 95th Street, the trail loop west of Spears Woods is hilly and challenging, winding west to a newer trail section known as the Old Country Lane. It heads south from 87th Street all the way to 107th Street.

This wide open lane also passes through Country Lane Woods off 95th Street. Numerous footpaths and unofficial trails are evident throughout the preserves; riders must stay on established trails at all times to prevent damage to the natural area. The Sag Valley Division trails are south of the Calumet Sag Channel and Route 83.

The longer trail system is located between Route 83 and McCarthy Road.

A convenient access point and parking area is at Horsetail Lake on the east side of 104th Avenue, just north of McCarthy Road. This trail system is less traveled than the Palos Forest Preserve trails but is in more isolated areas with more perennial stream crossings and a great view of the toboggan slides off Route 83 between 96th Avenue and 104th Avenue.

The trail passes through open fields and densely wooded areas. At the easternmost loop trail, west of Palos Park Woods, the trail crosses a major ford, which can be impassable during high water or flash floods. West of 104th Avenue the trail loop becomes a one-way trail with a spur trail going north to Route 83 and another spur trail meandering west to Will-Cook Road. Generally, the spur trail sections are less traveled. A convenient parking area is at Horsetail Lake. This trail system totals 12.5 miles.

A smaller, separate trail system at Sag Valley is south of McCarthy Road or the Will-Cook Road. It is 5.75 miles and is a small loop around Tampier Slough. It becomes a one-way trail meandering south and west paralleling 135th Street to Wolf Road. This is the least traveled trail system within the Palos and Sag Valley Forest Preserves.

The entire trail system throughout the Palos and Sag Valley Forest Preserves offer one of the largest and most diversified natural areas available for mountain bike riding. Throughout the system, the rider will be exposed to hilly and forested terrain, beautiful meadows, many lakes, ponds, and sloughs, a great variety of wildlife, and bountiful fishing. The woodland areas provide colorful autumn foliage.

Facilities: Numerous parking areas and trail shelters exist throughout the Palos and Sag Valley Forest Preserves. Picnic and shelter areas have drinking water, latrines, and necessary parking.

Park Rules and Regulations: Ride single file, keeping to the right side of the trail. Stay in your own lane. Give warning before passing other trail users. Obey all stop signs. No speed or racing permitted. Bicyclists yield to hikers and equestrians. Give notice before passing other trail users. Do not ride on unpaved trails when the trail is muddy. Motor vehicles prohibited. For rider's safety, helmets are suggested.

Hours Open: Sunrise to sunset

Mailing Address and Phone Number: Forest Preserve District of Cook County, 536 North Harlem Avenue, River Forest, IL 60305; 708-771-1330; or Palos Division Headquarters, 708-839-5617, or Sag Valley Headquarters, 708-448-8532

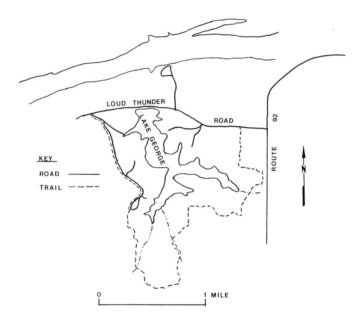

KEY

ROAD ———

TRAIL - - -

LOUD THUNDER ROAD

LAKE GEORGE

ROUTE 92

N

0   1 MILE

Loud Thunder Forest Preserve

30. Loud Thunder Forest Preserve

Trail Length: 6.5 miles

Trail Surface: Dirt, grass, park road

County: Rock Island

Location: Loud Thunder Forest Preserve is located in Rock Island County, southwest of the City of Rock Island. To reach the park take I-280 to Route 92, exit 11A. Head south on Route 92 for 12 miles, going past Andalusia, to Loud Thunder Road or Rock Island TT. Go west on this road 1.5 miles, past Lake George, to the park entrance, where the ranger residence house, boat concession, and horse campground are located.

Trail Description: The Sac Fox Trail may be started near the horse corral and campgrounds. At the south end of the campground is a small chain to pass by; then the trail heads through an open field for a short distance into a wooded area. The trail is marked with orange trail blazes and some small trail markers.

The trail starts out as a single lane and shortly goes down a small hill and over a small creek. The trail then starts making its way up hill and coming out in a large open field. Follow the grass field to the right, go past the first trail blaze you run across, and continue until you see a dirt road and fence going to another open field. Shortly beyond this, you will see the main trail with some trail blazes. This part of the trail goes up and down the hills and over the creek a few times. After crossing a main feeder creek for the lake, the trail will climb up a hill, go through a wooded area, and then come out to a wide grass lane. Turn left on this lane and follow it. You are now going through a Boy Scout Camp area and you will see some scout signs. Stay on this lane, going north and then east. The trail will ultimately

Bridge crossing, Loud Thunder Forest Preserve

come to the scouting area where you will see numerous buildings. Just past the swimming pool, you will see the trail head back into the woods. This is a nice trail here since it is well maintained between the two scouting sites. A small bridge crosses over to the second scouting area.

The trail goes to the right past a metal building and an archery range, and then into the woods and up a hill. At the top of the hill is a small clearing. The trail continues into a wooded area, goes up and down a few small hills and over a small creek, parallels an open field, and comes out at Loud Thunder Road. A car pullout and a sign for Loud Thunder is found at the road. Follow Loud Thunder Road west back to the park road, which goes all the way back then to the horse campground. On the north side of Loud Thunder Road is the Hauberg Trail and another spur of the Sac-Fox Trail. These trails are for hiking only; no biking, horseback riding, or motorized vehicles are allowed on these trail segments.

Trail marker, Loud Thunder Forest
Preserve

Facilities: Loud Thunder Forest Preserve has 1600 acres
as well as the 167-acre Lake George and borders the
Mississippi River on the north. A small campground
and boat launch are found along the Mississippi River.
Numerous picnic facilities, picnic tables, water and
restrooms, playground equipment, a few campgrounds,
a boat rental, and concession stand are available. Fishing is allowed in Lake George and the Mississippi River.

Park Rules and Regulations: Swimming is not allowed
in Lake George. The camping limit is 14 days. Gas motors arc prohibited in Lake George. All pets must be

kept on a leash. Fires are allowed only in designated picnic and camping areas. No hunting or firearms, or bows and arrows are allowed in the forest preserve. The destruction or cutting of any trees or vegetation is prohibited.

Hours Open: The park hours are 6:00 A.M. to 10:00 P.M. After 10:00 P.M. only registered campers are allowed in the forest preserve.

Mailing Address and Phone Number: Loud Thunder Forest Preserve, Illinois City, IL 61259; 309-795-1040

31. Hennepin Canal State Trail

Trail Length: 78 miles, one way

Trail Surface: Dirt, grass, limestone screenings, asphalt

Counties: Bureau, Henry, Rock Island, and Whiteside

Location: The Hennepin Canal main trail goes from the Mississippi River near Rock Island to Bureau Junction on the Illinois River. The feeder canal goes from Rock Falls south for 29 miles, joining the main canal, west of the Visitor's Center. Currently both the main canal and the feeder canal are open to mountain bike riding. The entire main canal may be ridden, although the Illinois Department of Natural Resources recommends that bicyclists ride between Lock 8 on the east and Lock 26 on the west, because of canal construction activities, for a distance of 48.7 miles. Rather than stopping at Lock 8 you can go to Lock 6 where there is a day use area. Check with the site superintendent for details concerning traveling past Lock 6. To reach the parking area along the feeder canal, travelers may take Route 40 into Rock Falls. Take Route 40 north to Dixon Avenue. Turn east on Dixon and proceed over the canal to Emmons Road, where there is a sign for the trail and boat launch. Go north on Emmons Road to Second Street. Past Second Street will be the parking area for Government Dam along the Rock River (Sinnissippi Lake) and the start of the Hennepin Feeder Canal. To reach Lock 8 area, take State Route 29 north from Peoria or west out of La Salle to 910 N. Turn west on 910 N and proceed for 5 miles to 2050 E. Turn north onto 2050 E and go a few blocks to the canal. There is no parking area here, but there is room to park next to the canal.

    To reach Lock 26, travelers can take I-80 to exit 19, Route 82. Proceed 1 mile north on Route 82 to Route 6. Turn west on Route 6 and proceed for 6 miles to 900 E.

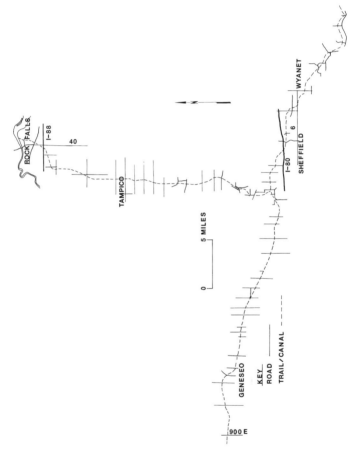

Hennepin Canal State Trail. Redrawn from Illinois Department of Transportation County Highway maps.

Rider along the Hennepin Canal

Turn north and proceed 1 mile to the canal. Parking is on the left side of the road, on the south side of the canal. To reach the Visitors Center near Sheffield, take I-80 to Illinois Route 40. Travel south on Route 40 for 1 mile. A sign along the road marks the Hennepin Canal Visitors Center. Turn west on this road and proceed 1 mile to the Visitors Center parking lot, and the canal.

Trail Description: The Hennepin Canal State Trail follows the towpath of the historic, Hennepin Canal. The canal was used from 1907 until 1951 for navigation. It was constructed between 1890 and 1907. In the early 1970s the canal was transferred to the former Illinois Department of Conservation for recreational use. Today it is a marvelous trail network and greenway. It is also part of the American Discovery Trail, which is the proposed trail network across the country, and the Grand Illinois Trail, a 475-mile loop trail and roadway network crossing northern Illinois, that the Illinois Department of Natural Resources and the Rails-to-Trails Conservancy, Illinois Chapter, are promoting.

The Hennepin Canal State Trail is a multipur-

Locktender's house in Wyanet, Hennepin Canal

pose trail shared by bicyclists, hikers, horseback riders, snowmobilers, cross-country skiers, and even canoeists. It is an excellent linear trail network and a challenging ride. In fact, this is the longest trail system for the rider in this book.

The trail follows the towpath most of the length of the canal, and most of the roads and bridges are marked. As mentioned earlier, the canal trail may be ridden from west to east, or east to west, along the main canal, or along the feeder from Rock Falls to the main canal. The trail is very strenuous, even on flat terrain. The uneven surfaces, different soil types, as well the length, make the ride a challenge. At the western end, the trail for all practical purposes, stops at 900 E because 2.5 miles farther on is the Green River, which can no longer be crossed.

All along the entire trail network, the rider will run across numerous locks, aqueducts, truss bridges, lock-tenders's homes, day-use areas, the Visitors Center, and prairies. It also goes near the birth place of former President Ronald Reagan, in Tampico. An excellent concentration of locks is also found in Wyanet, east of the Visi-

Trailhead at Hennepin feeder canal, Rock River

tors Center. The trail follows both sides of the canal on the main canal, while it is on the west side of the feeder canal. The feeder canal starts out as an asphalt trail for the first 3 miles through Rock Falls. An excellent view of Government Dam and a locktenders home is seen here. After the asphalt section, the trail surface is limestone screening all the way to Route 92.

Numerous parking areas and a few boat launches are found in this stretch. A side trip may also be made to Tampico, which is about 1.5 miles west of the canal along 300 N.

South of Route 92 for the rest of the feeder, as well as the remainder of the main canal, the canal is either grass or dirt. This part of the feeder canal may be extremely challenging to the rider since it is not maintained as well as the other segments and it is a grass path. An aqueduct carries the canal over the Green River, where there is prairie. At the main canal is a large pool of water known as the summit pool. Water from here heads west to the Mississippi River and east to the Illinois River. Bikers must ride west along the main canal on the north side of the canal to the first bridge to reach the south side of the main canal.

Tunnel under road, Hennepin Canal

Heading east from the feeder, the main trail parallels the south side of the canal to 645 E. Cross the bridge
at 645 E and then follow the north side of the canal. The
trail then heads toward I-80, where the trail riding is a
little bit rough. Just before the Visitors Center, cross
Bridge 15 to the Visitors Center, a complex that houses
a small museum offering some historical facts on how
the canal was built and some information on local wildlife. Park brochures and information can be picked up
here. Water and restrooms are also found here, as well
as a small fishing pond. Heading east past the Visitors
Center, the trail stays on the south side of the canal,
passes by a few bridges, and then just past Route 6/34
is Lock 21 Day-Use Area and some camping sites. You
will ride by a concrete boat repair foundation. Near Wyanet, five locks, an aqueduct, and a locktender's house
are found within a few miles. It's a nice place to take a
break and to ride into town for some refreshments.

A few day-use areas are encountered heading east
as well as some more bridges. Locks 8 and 7 are found
near 2050 E and Lock 6 is near 2160 E. Heading west
from the feeder canal, the trail will pass by Lock 22,
which is a day-use area, and then Lock 23 at 1920 E. An

aqueduct is crossed and then Lock 24 is on the outskirts of Geneseo. Found here is Ikes Park, where camping is allowed and there is a boat slip. This is also a good area for a break and a place to get some water.

Toward the west is another aqueduct to cross, Bridge 39, where there is a boat ramp, and shortly one will come out to 900 E. Riders can continue to the Green River, where the trail terminates. Found along the entire canal are nice wooded segments with some large cottonwoods and numerous bird species. Often you may be the only person along the beautiful canal, but in some spots many people also fish and boat the canal.

Facilities: Numerous picnic facilities are found, as well as camping areas, boat launches, and the Visitors Center. For additional park information request the Feeder, Western Branch, and Eastern Branch brochures, canal maps, a pamphlet on distances along the canal, as well as the general park pamphlet. Separate canoe and horseback brochures are also available.

Park Rules and Regulations: No motorcycles or fires allowed on the trail. Pets must be on a leash. Horseback riding limited on some trail segments. No camping at the Visitors Center.

Hours Open: The Visitors Center is open Monday through Friday from 8:00 A.M. until 4:00 P.M., and Saturday, Sunday, and holidays from 10:00 A.M. until 4:00 P.M.

Mailing Address and Phone Number: Hennepin Canal Parkway State Park, R.R. 2, Box 201, Sheffield, IL 61361; 815-454-2328

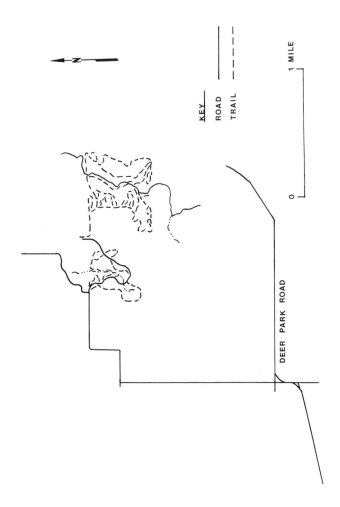

KEY

ROAD ——————

TRAIL – – – –

0 ⊢———————⊣ 1 MILE

DEER PARK ROAD

N

Catlin Park of La Salle County

32. Catlin Park of La Salle County

Trail Length: 13 miles

Trail Surface: Dirt, grass

County: La Salle

Location: Catlin Park is located east of Starved Rock State Park. To reach the park, travelers can take I-39 to exit 48 for Tonica. Turn east on County Road 14, to N 2101 Road. Take N 2101 for 4 miles to Route 178. Turn north on Route 178 and go 1 mile to Deer Park Road. Turn east on Deer Park Road and follow this road for 5 miles until you see the sign for Catlin Park. Turn north on this gravel road and go 2.5 miles to the park entrance.

Trail Description: Catlin Park has 13 miles of beautiful multipurpose trails for hikers, bikers, and horseback riders. The trails can be started at the park entrance or at the large barn at the end of the park road, where there is a trailboard.

The trail system is broken into two separate parts, one to the east of the barn and one to the west. The trails east are more secluded and are longer than the west set of trails. Each trail is marked with color-coded signs, and both are generally wide enough for a vehicle to pass through.

Heading east from the barn the trail parallels an open field. From here the trail heads south and then a series of loop trails join the main trail periodically. The loop trails are wooded and hilly. There are a few small creeks to cross and a large shelter is seen along one of the loop trails. The main trail ultimately winds its way to the south end of the property, goes down a hill, and crosses two small streams. The second stream crossing could be a challenge if water is high.

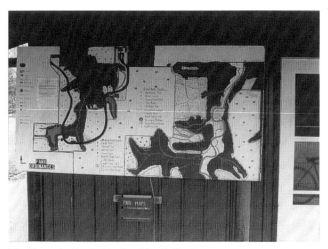

Trailboard, Catlin Park of La Salle County

Beyond the second stream, the trail, an old road bed, goes uphill and comes out to a field where there are signs for the south loop and the back forty loop. The south loop is short. The back forty loop goes by an open field, and at the north end, it joins a connecting trail that heads west toward the first set of loops on the west side of the creek.

Some of the hills leading down to the floodplain are steep. The east trails are all wooded, and there are some beautiful old oaks in the area. Wildlife such as deer as well as wild turkey and numerous other bird species may be seen.

The trails on the west side of the park wind their way around the picnic areas and some shelters. The main trail parallels the park road, goes by the fishing pond, comes out by the front gate, and then meanders through the woods. The trail through the woods is more secluded and goes into a small stream valley, crossing the creek numerous times. It ultimately winds its way east and comes out to the road back to the trailhead.

Near the east trailhead, there are some fenced-in areas that are home to various species of animals.

Facilities: Catlin Park has picnic facilities, shelters, fishing ponds, water, and restrooms.

Park Rules and Regulations: All motorized vehicles are restricted to the main road and parking lots.

Hours Open: The park is open 9:00 A.M. until 7:00 P.M., May 1 until October 1 each year. The park is closed November 1 until April 30.

Mailing Address and Phone Number: La Salle County Parks Department (Catlin Park of La Salle County), R.R. 4, 2560 E 1251 St. Road, Ottawa, IL 61350; 815-434-0518

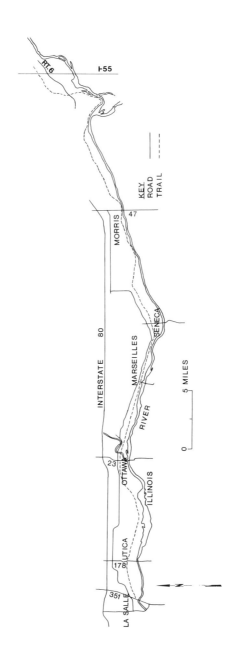

Illinois and Michigan Canal Trail. Redrawn from Illinois Department of Transportation Highway maps.

33. Illinois and Michigan Canal Trail

Trail Length: 55.5 miles, one way

Trail Surface: Limestone screenings, gravel

Counties: Will, Grundy, and La Salle

Location: The Illinois and Michigan Canal Trail has many starting points. Some main beginning locations include Channahon, La Salle, and Utica. To reach Channahon State Park, take I-55. Southwest of Joliet, exit at Route 6 and go west to the town of Channahon. Turn south onto Canal Street in Channahon and proceed half a mile until you see the park signs. Turn right and go one block to the entrance. To reach Gebhard Woods State Park in La Salle, take I-80 or Route 6 and go to the intersection of Routes 6 and 47 in Morris. Go west on Route 6 five blocks to Union Street. Turn south on Union Street and follow the signs to the park entrance. To reach the trail in La Salle, follow Route 351 through La Salle. When you see Canal Street on the north side of the canal, turn west and go about 100 feet to a parking area on the south side of Canal Street. The trailhead in Utica may be reached by taking Route 178 into Utica. South of the canal, turn west onto Johnson Street and go three blocks to Morton Street. Turn north on Morton Street and proceed to the parking area.

Trail Description: The Illinois and Michigan Canal was the impetus for the settlement and development of northeastern Illinois. The canal was directly responsible for the beginning of Chicago's growth as well as the cause for the development of Lockport, Joliet, Morris, Seneca, Marseilles, Ottawa, Utica, and La Salle-Peru. The Illinois and Michigan Canal actually had its origin with the Indians at the Chicago portage, the low divide between the waters of Lake Michigan and the Des

Locktender's house, lock 6, Illinois and Michigan Canal

Plaines River. The Indians used it as a land crossing spot long before the advent of Europeans. This portage was recorded in the annals of the French explorers Joliet and Marquette in 1673. It was also noted in 1790 by the French military engineer Victor Collot and in 1807 by U.S. Secretary of the Treasury Albert Gallatin in his report on roads and canals. The original boundary of Illinois was moved about 50 miles in order to give Illinois a coast on Lake Michigan and to ensure that Chicago, the point at which the canal would connect with Lake Michigan, would be in Illinois.

Construction of the canal was started by the State of Illinois in 1836 and was completed in 1848. The canal cost about $9.5 million, stretched 96 miles, and linked Lake Michigan with the Illinois River at La Salle, the two bodies of water from which the canal took its name. When the canal was originally built, it was 36 feet wide at the bottom, 60 feet wide at water level, and had a 15-foot wide towpath. The canal included fifteen locks, three dams, and four aqueducts. Several feeder streams, two with aqueducts, once fed the canal. Today,

Bike/pedestrian bridge over Du Page River, Illinois and Michigan Canal

some of the locks and aqueducts may be seen while riding.

On January 1, 1974, the canal was transferred to the Department of Conservation for the development of a hiking and biking trail. In addition, about 28 miles of the canal are filled with water for canoeing.

In February 1984, Congress established the Illinois and Michigan Canal Heritage Corridor. The act created a 100-mile linear historical park system with a commission to see that the corridor is preserved. The goals are to protect and enhance the cultural, natural, and recreational resources along the Illinois and Michigan Canal Corridor.

There are approximately 55.5 miles of marked biking trails along the Illinois and Michigan Canal State Trail. Along the trails, there are various state parks, parking lots, roads, and towns, where the rider can get to the trail. In addition, these trail access points may serve as starting or ending points for the rider. Since the trail is linear, bikers must backtrack or set up a vehicle or ride at the other end of the trail. Although the rider may go the entire length of the canal, not all segments

Lock 7, Illinois and Michigan Canal

of the canal have water in them. In fact, not even half of the canal has water anymore. Water is not found in the canal from the east side of Utica all the way to the spillway, 1.5 miles west of Gebhard Woods State Park. For nice views of the canal with water in it, we recommend doing the trail segments from Channahon State Park to the spillway west of Gebhard Woods State Park, or the segment from Utica to Lock 14 in La Salle, Illinois.

From the Channahon Access Area, the trail crosses over a creek and goes to Lock 6 and the locktender's house. Heading east, the trail goes past residential homes, crosses Knapp Street, and parallels a road for a short distance. This area of the canal is tree lined with lots of bird life. The trail comes to a locked gate at the frontage road off I-55, where currently (1996), the trail ends. Heading west from Lock 6, the rider crosses over a bridge over the Du Page River and will go past Lock 7. Nice views of the river are had here. Across Bridge Street, a parking area is found right next to the canal. A trailboard set up at the parking area gives the trail distances for four locations: McKinley Woods, 2.8 miles; Dresden Access, 5.8 miles; Aux Sable Access, 8.1 miles; and Gebhard Woods, 14.8 miles.

Past Bridge Street, the trail heads south with the canal on the right and shortly the Des Plaines River appearing on the left side. At McKinley Woods you will see a small wooden bridge that goes over the canal, leading to the woods. Picnic facilities, car parking, and a shelter are found at McKinley Woods.

From here, the trail goes west. Prior to reaching Dresden Lock and Dam, you will see a sign for a camping and picnic area on the left side of the trail. There you will see some picnic tables, a small wooden shelter with a fireplace in it, and restrooms. Just beyond the camping area, you will pass Dresden Lock and Dam, which has a rest bench. Approximately 2 miles farther, you will arrive at Aux Sable Access. Before reaching this access point, you will pass another camping area. Beyond the camping area, the trail crosses a road and then comes to the access area. Another lock and dam and an aqueduct can be seen at this access. A parking lot, water pump, and restrooms are also available at this access. In addition, a small wooden bridge, which allows you to view the lock and dam system, goes over the lock and dam.

Past the Aux Sable Access Area, cross a bridge over the canal and follow the towpath on the south side again. In a few miles you will see many residential homes on the north side of the canal. At this point, the trail is at the outskirts of Morris. The trail goes by William G. Stratton State Park and then crosses a bridge to the north side of the canal. Prior to reaching Gebhard Woods State Park, you will see the Nettle Creek Aqueduct. From this point you may continue following the towpath a short distance to the park, or you may follow the trail and paint blazes away from the canal to the camping and picnic areas within the park, or head west along the trail.

Head west past Gebhard Woods State Park and follow the south side of the canal. About 2.5 miles farther, the water from the canal goes over a small spillway and flows toward the Illinois River. Shortly beyond this location the canal is dry, and for the most part remains dry all the way to Utica. Although the canal has no water in it past the spillway, there are some very nice wooded stretches along the canal. Between the spillway and the outskirts of Seneca, the trail is all gravel and wooded. A good variety of birds may be seen in this section.

At the edge of Seneca, the trail becomes a gravel road. In Seneca, you will see an old grain elevator next to the canal with a sign that reads, "John Armour's warehouse erected in 1861–62. This building is the earliest grain elevator along the canal." West of Seneca, the trail follows a gravel road, goes through some wooded areas and by some farms, and then becomes a part of the road. On the east side of Marseilles, the trail goes past various industries and chemical plants. The trail goes through Marseilles, where Locks 9 and 10 (dry) are, and then continues heading through town. Then for the most part it parallels Route 51. The trail along this segment also goes through many wooded areas.

On the east side of Ottawa, the trail crosses the Fox River over the Fox River Aqueduct, which affords a good view of the river and town. The trail then continues through the center of town.

Five miles outside of town is Buffalo Rock State Park, where there are five earthenware sculptures of aquatic animals native to the area. These sculptures were created from the spoil material left as a result of coal mining operations.

The next 5-mile ride from Buffalo Rock State Park to the edge of Utica has some nice wooded areas. At the edge of Utica is a spillway that drains part of the canal containing water. In Utica, on the north side of the canal, is the La Salle County Historical Museum, an 1848 warehouse that preserves artifacts of the area and offers information on the canal. The trail then passes through town; a little way beyond one will have good views of the Illinois River backwaters on the left side. Bluffs are seen on the right side of the canal, and one rock formation is named Split Rock. In La Salle, at Lock 14, are some stairs on the north side of the canal which take you to a parking area. Lock 14 was restored in 1981–82. Past Lock 14, the Illinois and Michigan Canal joins the Illinois River.

Facilities: Gebhard Woods State Park has picnic facilities with tables, grills, water, restrooms, and a shelter. A baseball diamond and horseshoe pits are also available. Children may fish in the four ponds in the park. Youth camping sites are also available.

Channahon State Park has picnic tables, shelters, restrooms, water, grills, and playground equipment. Tent camping is also available. Locks 6 and 7 and the locktender's house at Lock 6 are found at Channahon State Park. Fishing is allowed in the canal and in the Du Page, the Illinois, and the Des Plaines rivers, contingent upon all Illinois fishing rules and regulations.

Park Rules and Regulations: Pets must be on leash at all times. See specific park brochures.

Hours Open: Gebhard Woods, Buffalo Rock, and Channahon State Parks are open year-round except on Christmas Day and New Year's Day. When weather conditions necessitate the closing of roads during freezing and thawing periods, access to the park or facilities is by foot only.

Mailing Addresses and Phone Numbers: Gebhard Woods State Park, 101 Ottawa, Morris, IL 60450; 815-942-9669; Channahon State Park, P.O. Box 54, Channahon, IL 60410; 815-467-4271; or Buffalo Rock State Park, P.O. Box 39, Ottawa, IL 61350; 815-433-2220

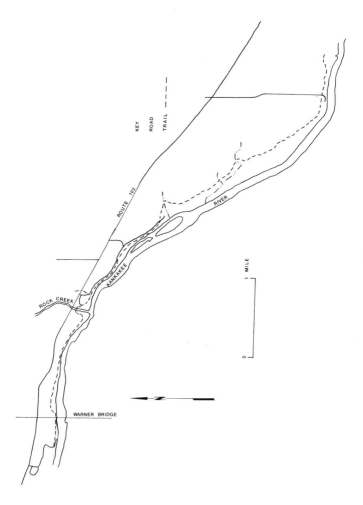

KEY

ROAD ————

TRAIL — — —

ROUTE 102

KANKAKEE RIVER

ROCK CREEK

1 MILE

0

N

WARNER BRIDGE

Kankakee River State Park

34. Kankakee River State Park

Trail Length: 7.5 miles, one way

Trail Surface: Limestone screenings, pavement

Counties: Kankakee, Will

Location: Kankakee River State Park is located west of Kankakee. From I-57, take exit 315 to Route 50 south. Go 1.5 miles to Armour Road, and turn west. Follow Armour Road for a short distance to Route 102. Turn northwest on Route 102 and proceed northwest for almost 5 miles to the park entrance. Travelers on I-55 can take exit 241, Wilmington, to River Road. Follow River Road east for about 4 miles to Route 53. Turn south at Route 53 and go to Route 102 in downtown Wilmington. Turn east on Route 102 and travel 13 miles to the park entrance on the south side of Route 102.

Trail Description: The Kankakee River State Park Bicycle Trail has several starting locations within the park, but a good place to begin is near the park office, where there is a small parking area. Directly across the park road is the trail. The trail is a 6–8-foot-wide limestone-screened trail, going from the Davis Creek Group area on the east all the way to the parking area just west of Warner Bridge Road.

The trail goes by the Kankakee River near the park office, where there are scenic views. Heading northwest along the river, one will see some viewing platforms looking out over the river. The trail then goes over a nice little wooden bridge, passes by the concession stand, and then comes to a suspension bridge over Rock Creek. A beautiful view of Rock Creek and the small canyon can be observed from this bridge.

The trail continues through a small wooded area, paralleling the river, then goes along the river's edge and

Suspension bridge over Rock Creek, Kankakee River State Park

under the Warner Road Bridge. The trail ends at a parking area and canoe launch.

Heading southeast from the park office, the trail parallels the park road for a short distance and goes over a few wooden bridges. It continues past the Potawatomi camping area and moves away from the river at this point into a nice wooded area. The trail then crosses a gravel road and comes out near the Davis Creek Group Area. A gravel road here leads down to the river.

Facilities: A staffed park office with maps and brochures, numerous picnic areas (with shelters, water, and restrooms), a few campgrounds, hiking, horseback and snowmobile trails, and a concession stand near Rock Creek are available. Canoeing is allowed on the Kankakee River, and fishing is allowed in the Kankakee River and Rock Creek. A nice hiking trail on the north side of Route 102 along Rock Creek takes you by a small waterfall.

Rock Creek Canyon, Kankakee River State Park

Trail/covered bridge, Kankakee River State Park

Park Rules and Regulations: No alcoholic beverages. No swimming in the Kankakee River or Rock Creek. Pets must be on a leash at all times. Keep vehicles off the grass. Motorized vehicles are prohibited on all of the Kankakee River State Park trails.

Hours Open: The park is open from 6:00 A.M. until 10:00 P.M. Office hours are from 10:00 A.M. until 4:00 P.M.

Mailing Address and Phone Number: Kankakee River State Park, P.O. Box 37, Bourbonnais, IL, 60914; 815-933-1383

35. Rock Island State Trail

Trail Length: 28.5 miles, one way

Trail Surface: Limestone screenings

Counties: Peoria and Stark

Location: Rock Island State Trail is located northwest of Peoria. The trail has two main trailheads, one in Alta and the other one on the outskirts of Toulon. The trail may be started or finished at either of these two locations.

To reach the trailhead in Alta, take the bypass (474) to Route 6. Follow Route 6 to Allen Road (exit 5). Proceed north on Allen Road to Alta. The main parking lot is 1 mile from Route 6 on the right side of the road. This parking area has a trailboard along with water, pit toilets, and a small picnic area. To reach the trailhead at Toulon, continue on the road through Alta to Route 91. Stay on Route 91 north for 38 miles, going through the towns of Dunlap, Princeville, and Wyoming, all the way to the east side of Toulon. On the north side of the road is another sign for Rock Island parking. This parking area has water, toilets, and a small picnic area.

Trail Description: In the late 1950s the Chicago, Rock Island, and Pacific Railroad ceased operation along its track running from Peoria to Toulon. In subsequent years the tracks, ties, some ballasts, drainage structures, and bridge components were salvaged and removed from the right-of-way. The Department of Conservation undertook a study to evaluate the potential of the Rock Island trail as a multiple-use linear recreation corridor. It was determined that the Rock Island trail would provide needed recreational opportunities for the region and state. Over the years many obstacles have impeded the development of the trail. These included adjoining

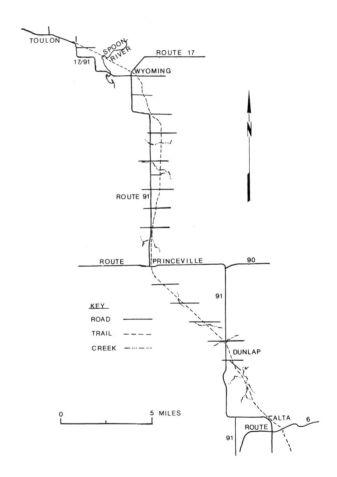

Rock Island State Trail. Redrawn from Illinois Department of
Transportation Highway maps.

landowners' objections to any development and lack of funding for the project.

In 1989 development of the Rock Island State Trail was initiated. It included trail markings, a campground, and trail surfacing. The trail was completed at the end of 1989 and is now open to riders, hikers, and skiers. The Rock Island State Trail is now a 28.5-mile, one-way, linear trail. Bikers who plan to ride the entire length or a partial segment of the trail will have to leave a vehicle at the other end of the trail or have someone pick them up.

The trail is very well marked with trailboards as well as mile markers. One will also see bridge warning signs, stop signs by roads, and bicycle signs through the towns of Dunlap, Princeville, and Wyoming. The entire trail is also laid down with compacted limestone.

From Alta south, the trail crosses Alta Road (be careful here), goes through a small wooded area, and heads down a hill toward Route 6. A bike tunnel under Route 6 will have to be used. Bicyclists are prohibited from riding in this tunnel. On the other side, the trail winds its way along a creek and goes by the outskirts of an airport. The trail comes to an active railroad line, and parallels the airport. The trail then parallels the existing railroad line all the way to Pioneer Parkway. This part of the trail is run by the Peoria Park District, which plans to connect this trail with the Pimiteoui Trail in Peoria and eventually to trails in East Peoria and Morton. Heading north from Alta, bikers can enjoy some tree-lined canopy. Within 2 miles there is a sign for the Kickapoo Creek Recreation Area. This is an area for picnicking and primitive camping. Tables, grills, water, and toilets are found here. Shortly beyond this area, the trail crosses over Kickapoo Creek to a beautiful view of the creek valley below. Follow the bicycle signs along the road when passing through Dunlap. Between Dunlap and Princeville the trail is generally uneventful, going by farms and a few small wooded tracts.

The trail then comes to the southern part of Princeville and goes through the center of town following the bicycle signs. At the north end of town is a sign that directs the biker off the road and back onto the old railroad grade. This is mile 11 at this point. Between Princeville and Wyoming the rider will go by a nature preserve and a small parking lot. This is found at County Line Road 00N. Past this area the rider will cross two small creeks, Mud Run and Camp Run creeks. Camp Run Creek is near mile 16. At the outskirts of Wyoming, the rider will see the old Chicago, Burlington, and Quincy Railroad Depot. This is a nice spot for a break and for some photo opportunities. The trail then goes through town, following the bicycle signs again to the trailhead at the other end of town. There are a few stores in town, should the rider be interested in stopping for some refreshments. The stretch between Wyoming and Toulon is very pretty, especially over the Spoon River. The trail goes over a wooden bridge here, and it is worth the time to stop here and rest for a while to view the Spoon River Valley below. Beyond the Spoon River, the trail heads west, and in 3 miles it terminates at the parking lot on the outskirts of Toulon.

Facilities: The facilities along the trail include benches and the Kickapoo Creek Recreation Area facilities. In addition, as previously stated, there are a few items at the trailheads. Facilities such as restaurants, stores, and so forth are available in Dunlap, Princeville, and Wyoming, as well as in Alta and Toulon.

Park Rules and Regulations: No motorized vehicles allowed on the trail. Dogs must be on a leash.

Hours Open: The trail is open sunrise to sunset, year-round.

Mailing Address and Phone Number: Rock Island Trail State Park, P.O. Box 64, Wyoming, IL 61491; 309-695-2228; or Peoria Park District, 2218 North Prospect Road, Peoria, IL 61603-2193; 309-682-1200

36. Jubilee College State Park

Trail Length: 25 miles

Trail Surface: Dirt, grass

County: Peoria

Location: To reach Jubilee College State Park, take I-74 west out of Peoria to exit 82. Turn north on this road and go 1 mile to the town of Kickapoo. Turn west at U.S. Route 150 and proceed 3 miles to the park entrance, located on the right side of the road. Watch for a sign for Jubilee College State Park.

Trail Description: The trail system at Jubilee College consists of more than 25 miles of multipurpose trails winding around the park and on both sides of Jubilee Creek. These trails are used by bikers, hikers, horseback riders, and cross-country skiers. They are well traveled and offer a variety of riding terrain. The trails are marked with various trail markers such as a multipurpose trail marker, hiker sign, or a horseshoe.

The area along the Jubilee Creek floodplain can be muddy and overgrown during the wet season. A good place to start the trail system is at the day-use area. This picnic area, just east of the campground, has 4 picnic sites—Quail Meadow, Red Fox Run, Prairie Lane, and Bow Wood Glen. There is one trailboard behind the Quail Meadow shelter next to the trail and another on the north side of the park road near the open field. These trailboards may be a little outdated, and it is wise to get an up-to-date trail map.

The trails along the south side of Jubilee Creek but north of the park road, wind their way in the floodplain area going up and down a few small hills. Near the campground area the trail goes by a fishing pond, up a hill, and then parallels the camping area and road.

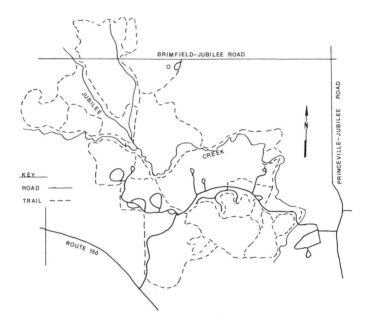

KEY

ROAD ⸺

TRAIL - - -

Jubilee College State Park. Redrawn from park map. Map not drawn to scale.

Creek crossing, Jubilee College State Park

It veers south toward the park entrance following an old gravel road for a short distance, through a wooded area, then crosses the park road where it continues along a southern boundary line through an open prairie, and finally into a wooded area. The trail then connects with a network of trails south of the day-use area. This is a really great area for riding, as the trail system winds up and down hills and goes through beautiful wooded areas, stream valleys, and open prairies. This area is the more popular among mountain bike riders.

The trail system then crosses the park road at a few locations, making its way through the woods, down the hill back to the floodplain of Jubilee Creek. There are numerous trail crossings of Jubilee Creek. Most of the horseback riders will be north of the creek, since they make their way from the equestrian campground. The trails in this area wind up and down the small hills and cross some small perennial streams. Be careful when crossing Jubilee Creek, especially when the current is swift or muddy. Bike riders should also give the right of way to horseback riders.

The local bike club sponsors mountain bike races at Jubilee College State Park.

Trailboard, Jubilee College State Park

Facilities: Jubilee College State Park has numerous picnic areas, shelters, water, restrooms, and campgrounds.

Park Rules and Regulations: Pets must be on a leash.

Hours Open: Jubilee College State Park is open 8:00 A.M. until 10:00 P.M. The park office hours are from 9:00 A.M. until 1:00 P.M. The campgrounds are closed from November 1 until April 15.

Mailing Address and Phone Number: Jubilee College State Park, 13921 W. Route 150, Brimfield, IL 61517; 309-446-3758

37. Farmdale Recreation Area

Trail Length: 4+ miles

Trail Surface: Dirt

County: Tazewell

Location: Farmdale Recreation Area is located in East Peoria. To reach the site, travelers can take I-74 to exit 95C, Route 150/8, east. Follow Route 150/8 until Route 150 splits off; take Route 8 (Washington Street) east to Farmdale Road. Proceed south on Farmdale Road to Summit Street, where there is a sign for Farmdale Reservoir. Follow Summit Street for 2 miles to the parking area beyond the dam.

Trail Description: The dam was built in 1959 to protect the lower-lying areas from flooding. The area is usually dry but during severe flooding, the dam is closed and the area acts as a flood storage reservoir. Within the recreation area there are more than 4 miles of trails and 700 additional acres of area to ride.

From the parking area north of the dam, the trail, a wide dirt lane, goes by a metal gate, making its way toward Farm Creek. You may have to ford across. Next you will come to a trail junction that takes you south toward the dam. By taking the first trail junction toward the dam, you will go through a farmed area, by some ridges on the left, and then into a wooded area and into a stream valley. You will have to cross the small creek a few times in this area. Soon the trail heads east and climbs up a hill where it ends in a farm field. From here you can backtrack to a trail spur at the bottom of the hill. This trail leg then crosses the stream, goes up hill passing by pine trees, and then comes to an open field.

The trail follows the edge of the open field before it

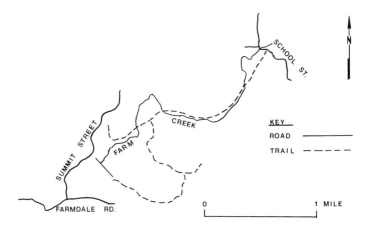

Farmdale Recreation Area

narrows and goes into a small wooded area, where some nice pine trees are found. Soon the trail makes its way toward the dam. The dam is restricted; no riding is allowed over it. If you go back to the first trailhead, the trail continues in the floodplain, going by a bluff line and then crossing Farm Creek again. The old trestles for a railroad are visible at both creek crossings. The trail is an old railroad bed now and begins to parallel the creek for a short distance.

An active railroad line appears in the near distance. Crossing over a concrete apron, the trail soon comes out to School Street, where there is a small parking area, locked gate, and a trailboard. From here, you can retrace the path or do some of your own blazing.

Facilities: There are restrooms at this recreation area.

Park Rules and Regulations: Pets must be under owner's control at all times. Hunting, open fires, operation of motorized vehicles, possession of any projectile firing device, cutting vegetation or disturbing the ground surface, being in a restricted area, and being in the area during hours of closure are all prohibited.

Hours Open: The park is open from sunrise to sunset.

Mailing Address and Phone Number: Park Ranger, U.S. Army Corps of Engineers, Foot of Grant Street, Peoria, IL 61603; 309-676-4601

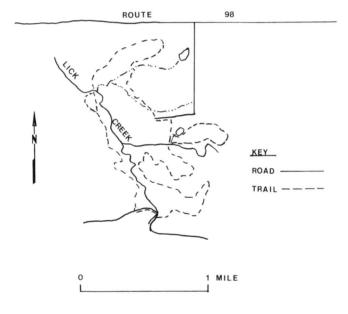

McNaughton Park

38. McNaughton Park

Trail Length: 7.4 miles

Trail Surface: Dirt, grass

County: Tazewell

Location: McNaughton Park is located on the north side of Pekin. To reach the park from the north or south take State Route 29 and turn east at State Route 98. Proceed 2 miles to the park entrance at County Road 1750 E or McNaughton Park Road. You may also take I-155 and turn off at Route 98, Birchwood Street (exit 31) and proceed 6.5 miles west to the park. Turn south on County Road 1750 E and go for 1 mile to the turn-around.

Trail Description: McNaughton Park was named after John T. McNaughton, who once owned the *Pekin Times* newspaper. The development of the trail in McNaughton Park was started in the summer of 1970 and was completed in the spring of 1971, with the help of hikers, Boy Scout Troop 194, and the Pekin Park District. Today the trail is multipurpose with bikers, hikers, and horseback riders sharing the trail. The trail in McNaughton Park, called the Potawatomi Trail, measures over 7 miles. The trail is blazed with red spray paint on the trees. There are mile markers found along the trail and the numbering system begins from the horse stables. The trail may be started near the end of the road where there is a turnaround and parking for vehicles.

From the parking area, the trail follows the road and then branches off north into the woods. It starts heading down a small wooded creek valley to a small wooden bridge. This creek is crossed numerous times in this valley. The trail then goes up a steep hill and comes

Bridge and rider, McNaughton Park

out to an open field where power lines are located. After crossing this field under the power lines, it makes its way back into the woods. Crossing another small creek valley by a second wooden bridge, the trail makes its way up a ridge and comes out west of the horse stables. From here the trail heads west through an open area where you will see a totem pole. Passing the pole, the trail goes under the power lines again and makes its way down a sandy hill toward the Lick Creek Valley, where there is a good view of the river valley. Shortly, the trail crosses Lick Creek, which is sometimes quite high during the wet season. From here the trail parallels the creek for a short time before it starts up some hills. Numerous other connecting trails are found in this stretch. This

Rider seen through field, McNaughton Park

part of the trail system, from Lick Creek to Sheridan Road, is very difficult since it goes up and down some extremely steep grades a few times. Beyond this hilly section, the trail comes back to the floodplain. At the south end, the trail makes its way uphill, passes by a golf course, and comes down some stairs (that's right: stairs!), to Sheridan Road. This last stretch has some nice wooded sections. Follow Sheridan Road eastward for a short distance and, soon after you pass Lick Creek, the trail, part of an old road, turns into the woods, where some stairs will have to be climbed. From here the trail soon skirts a few open fields and then heads west until it reaches the creek again. The trail continues to parallel the creek, going by a 40-foot eroded stream bank and moving uphill to another open field. The trail travels along the edge of this open field for a short distance and then crosses another creek.

The trail heads east paralleling the creek for a short distance, starts north and then west, passing an old house foundation. Finally it comes down to the south side of a small lake. A connecting trail here takes you south down the creek valley to the trail at the creek. The

Author (Walter Zyznieuski) at totem pole seen along trail, McNaughton Park

trail then goes around the south end of the lake and up a small hill to the car turnaround area.

Facilities: There are picnic facilities with picnic tables and restrooms available by the turnaround. A small shelter and observation are also at the lake.

Park Rules and Regulations: No alcoholic beverages, hunting, trapping, or swimming allowed. No vehicles on the grass and no one allowed on the ice. Speed limit is 20 mph driving in the park. No dumping or littering. No disturbing animals or plant life. No cutting trees and shrubs or picking wildflowers. No fires in areas not designated. Fishing allowed at Zuercher and Butterfield lakes only. Watch for pedestrians.

Hours Open: 6:00 A.M. until 10:00 P.M.

Mailing Address and Phone Number: Pekin Park District, 1701 Court Street, Pekin, IL 61554; 309-347-3178

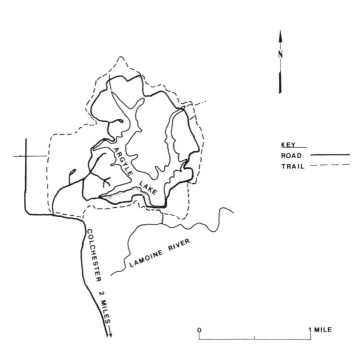

ARGYLE LAKE

COLCHESTER 2 MILES

LAMOINE RIVER

N

0   1 MILE

Argyle Lake State Park

39. Argyle Lake State Park

Trail Length: 7 miles

Trail Surface: Dirt, gravel

County: McDonough

Location: Argyle Lake State Park is located 7 miles west of Macomb and 2 miles north of Colchester. To reach the park, go 7 miles west of Macomb on State Route 136. In Colchester turn north on Coal Street and proceed 2 miles to the park entrance.

Trail Description: The mountain bike trail at Argyle Lake State Park is a shared horse trail 7 miles long. The trailhead begins at the horse campground, which is past the main entrance to the park where 1200 N intersects the road. Turn right here. A sign marks the Equestrian Trail. Found here are a barn, water, picnic tables, and a campground. There is a sign at the trailhead for the Horse Trail, and the trail is marked with a symbol of a rider on horseback.

Going around an open field, the trail winds its way into the woods as a single lane, heading down to a creek. It stays in the valley for a short distance. When it crosses the creek, there is a ravine to the right where the trail goes up the hill. The horse trail connects with the hiking trail on top of the hill and then splits off to the left. The trail parallels the hiking trail and park road.

Following a ridge top for a short time, the trail goes down to a creek valley and turns back toward the park road. Going down by a creek again and then up a hill, the trail crosses the hiking trail again, joining it for a short distance and then splitting off. At the top of the hill, the trail goes through some pine trees and at times may be difficult to follow. A short connecting trail leads to the park road in this section, where there is a trail-board.

The trail continues to wind its way around the lake, goes along a gravel road for a short distance, and then comes down below the dam where you will go right past the dam. From here the trail goes up the hill, winds its way through the woods, goes by a ravine, to come out at the edge of a field. Take the trail straight to the road and follow the road for three blocks to the park entrance road. Cross the road and follow the tree line back to the horse camp area.

Facilities: The park has numerous picnic facilities, such as tables, stoves, grills, water, restrooms, playground equipment, tent and trailer camping. A concession stand located on the lake offers a variety of refreshments and boats for rent. Fishing is allowed in the lake, contingent upon Illinois fishing rules and regulations.

Park Rules and Regulations: All vehicles must remain on the roadway, pets must be leashed, and swimming is prohibited.

Hours Open: The park is open every day except Christmas Day and New Year's Day from 6:00 A.M. until 10:00 P.M. The gates are closed at 11:00 P.M.

Mailing Address and Phone Number: Argyle Lake State Park, R.R. 1, Colchester, IL 62326; (309) 776-3422

40. Evergreen Lake, Comlara Park

Trail Length: 10 miles

Trail Surface: Dirt, grass, roads

Counties: McLean, Woodford

Location: Evergreen Lake, Comlara Park, is located north of Bloomington and Normal. To reach the park, take I-39 north to exit 8, Lake Bloomington Road or 2500 N. Take this road west 1 mile and turn south on County Road 33 at a sign for the park. Take this road a short distance to the park entrance on the right side of the road.

Trail Description: The trails at Comlara Park consist of 6 separate trails that wind around Evergreen Lake. The six trails connect with each other by short road segments between each trail. These six trails total more than 10 miles.

The trails are marked with signs, but on the west side of the lake they are marked with yellow or orange streamers. Trail segments are sometimes difficult to follow, because of the vegetation or lack of markers.

The trail starts behind the Visitors Center along the park road. It goes into the woods and toward the lake, paralleling the road. During the wet season the trail can be under water, and you may have to ride on higher ground.

The first trail, known as the Deer Island Area Access Trail, is 2.5 miles long. It goes all the way to 2300 N Road. A connecting spur is found at over a third of the way along this trail segment. The trail then goes through a wooded area, up and down a few small hills and parallel to the lake, coming out to 2300 N Road. Follow this road west to a home on the right side of the road. There is a chained gate here. This trail is known

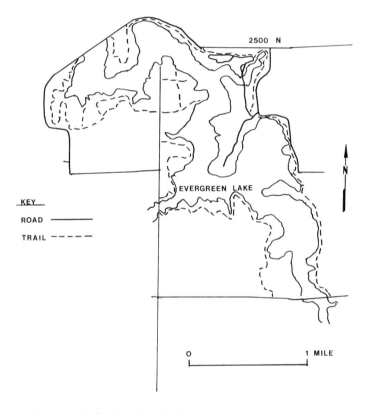

KEY

ROAD ——————

TRAIL ——————

2500 N

EVERGREEN LAKE

N

0   1 MILE

Evergreen Lake, Comlara Park

Evergreen Lake, Comlara Park

Bridge crossing, Evergreen Lake, Comlara Park

as the Southern Access Trail and is also 2.5 miles long. Follow it through a field, go over a small creek, and come out to another large field. The trail then follows the edge of the field for a third of its length, with an occasional streamer (trail marker) seen on a tree.

The trail then heads into the woods, where views of the lake and beach will be seen. At times, this trail segment is difficult to follow because of the lack of markers. Keep your eyes open for the streamers on the trees in this area. The trail then comes out by 1200 E, where a residential property is seen. Follow the road north to the Two Cedars Prairie Access Trail. This is a short trail that goes by a prairie and then by the lake, making its way back to 1200 E Road. Take 1200 E for a short distance to a small parking area on the right.

White Oak Access Trail, a short one that heads into the woods and down by the lake, goes north and winds its way back to 1200 E, where it comes out by the boat launch area. Restrooms, water, and picnic tables are found here. The road goes back south to the previous parking area, where the Lakeview Area Access Trail is found on the west side of the road.

This trail goes into the woods and then comes down to a section of the lake where there is a small

Evergreen Lake, Comlara Park

Trail sign, Evergreen Lake, Comlara
Park

floating bridge to cross. The trail then goes uphill where
it becomes an old road. There are some loop segments
as well as some trails leading down to the lake, and you
will pass a small parking area. Parts of the trail become
single lane in this area. The trail ultimately winds its
way toward the dam, where there are a few small
wooden bridges to cross. The trail comes out to the road
and then the biker follows the road going over the dam.
A good view of the spillway and lake is seen from the
dam. On the other side of the dam, the trail makes
its way back into the woods, going up a hill and then
following a peninsula. It goes underneath some power
lines and then heads back toward 2500 N Road, where
it parallels the road a short distance coming out near the
water pumping station.

Just past the pumping station, a path leads into

the campground area. The trail stays on the park road, heading to the east end of the campground to Campsite 60. Now it heads into the woods and goes down toward a stream. This is the Campers Park Access Trail.

The first leg on this trail is low lying. The second leg heads toward the park road, going on the edge of the woods and open fields. It then parallels the road and comes out near the Visitors Center, right by the gatehouse for the camping area.

Facilities: A campground with 130 campsites, is located here. Fishing is allowed in Evergreen Lake. A separate swimming facility is located on the lake. Boating is allowed with a maximum of 10 hp. There are picnic facilities, shelters, restrooms, and water.

Park Rules and Regulations: Swimming is prohibited except at the beach. Alcoholic beverages are prohibited. Unleashed pets are prohibited. Vehicles are prohibited on grass. Evergreen Lake watercraft registrations are required. Gathering of firewood is prohibited.

Hours Open: Quiet hours are from 10:00 P.M. until 8:00 A.M.

Mailing Address and Phone Number: McLean County Department of Parks and Recreation, R.R. 1, Comlara Park Road, Hudson, IL 61748; 309-726-2022

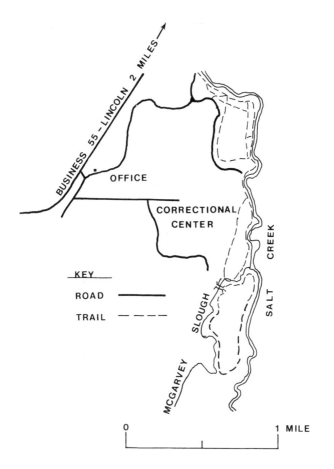

Edward R. Madigan State Park

41. Edward R. Madigan State Park

Trail Length: 7 miles

Trail Surface: Dirt, grass

County: Logan

Location: Edward R. Madigan State Park is located 2 miles south of Lincoln and borders Salt Creek. The park also surrounds the Lincoln and Logan Correctional centers. To reach the park, exit I-55 at Business 55 (exit 123) and go 1 mile to the state park sign. Turn right at the sign and go over the railroad tracks; the park is immediately to the left. The South Annex is to the right.

Trail Description: The Department of Conservation initially acquired 741 acres of land from the Department of Mental Health. The following year, park development began; currently there are 751 acres of land in the park. The park is named for the late Edward R. Madigan, former state senator, U.S. congressman, and secretary of the Department of Agriculture.

There are two trails in the park. The first is a short jogging trail located at the first parking facility. The other trail is a 7-mile multiple loop trail. The longest segment of the trail goes along Salt Creek and is known as the Salt Creek Trail. The trail can be reached from numerous points in the park. Maps of the park trail system can be obtained at the ranger's office, and trailboards are set up to show your location and the direction of the trail. The trail can be started by the cartop boat launch. From there it heads south, following Salt Creek and joining two other trail segments along the way. One of these trails branches west and parallels the park road, while the other trail parallels Salt Creek; this section of the trail may be inundated during the wet season. Both trails are about 10 feet wide, and during the winter months they are excellent ski trails. Parts of the trail along Salt Creek are washed out and the rider must be aware of these areas. The first washout is located just past the boat launch area.

The second one is found just past the canoe launch area and you will have to carry your bike for a short segment. The trail along Salt Creek soon branches west and parallels McGarvey Slough. A connecting trail leads up the hill to the South Annex parking area. The trail then crosses a bridge, passes by a small picnic area, and then does a small loop, passing by the largest sycamore tree in Illinois.

Return trail segments can then be taken back to the trailhead.

Facilities: A ranger station located in the park offers additional information. Picnic tables, grills, restrooms, drinking water, and shelters are also scattered throughout the park. Canoe and cartop boat launches are also located in the park. Salt Creek can be fished for large and smallmouth bass, bluegill, sunfish, crappie, catfish, bullheads, and carp. All appropriate Illinois fishing rules and regulations are in effect.

Park Rules and Regulations: No hunting allowed.

Hours Open: The park is open every day of the year except Christmas Day and New Year's Day. The park may be closed at certain times because of freezing and thawing, and one must enter on foot.

Mailing Address and Phone Number: Edward R. Madigan State Park, R.R. 3, Lincoln, IL 62656; 217-735-2424

42. Kickapoo State Park

Trail Length: 6+ miles

Trail Surface: Dirt, gravel

County: Vermilion

Location: Kickapoo State Park is located 6 miles west of Danville and 25 miles east of Champaign. To reach the park, travelers heading west on I-74 can take exit 210, where there is a sign for Kickapoo State Park. Follow this road for less than a mile, and then turn west on Henning Road. Proceed on Henning Road a mile and a half to County Road 32 and turn south. Follow this road 2 miles to the park. Travelers heading east on I-74 can take exit 206 and follow the signs for Kickapoo State Park. The park entrance is 3 miles from exit 206.

Trail Description: Direct evidence of prehistoric man's occupation of the Kickapoo area was uncovered by an archaeological excavation of a village site along the Middle Fork River a few miles north of the park. The Kickapoo Tribe had several villages just south of the park at the confluence of the Middle Fork and Salt Fork rivers near Vermilion salt springs.

The Vermilion salt springs located just southeast of the present park brought the first white settlement, called Salt Springs, to Vermilion County. An expedition led by Joseph Barren discovered the saline in 1819 and then returned to Fort Harrison. The first cabin at Salt Springs was constructed by several members of the party who remained behind to spend a miserable winter on the Salt Fork of the Vermilion River. Wells were dug to obtain the salt brine, which was then boiled in large rendering kettles to evaporate the water and obtain salt. The saltworks were run by a variety of different operators until 1848.

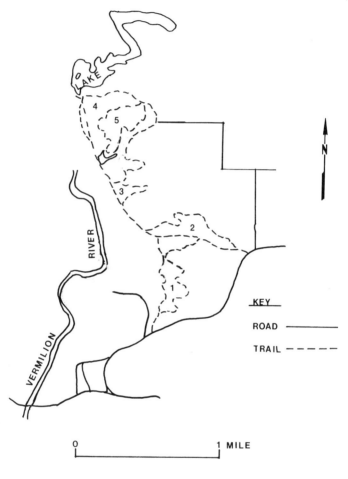

KEY
ROAD ————————
TRAIL — — — —

0   1 MILE

Kickapoo State Park

Trailhead, Kickapoo State Park

Today Kickapoo is an example of nature reclaiming its territory. At the turn of the century, about half of what is now the park was strip-mined for coal. These mining operations left the area with bare ridges of subsoil separated by deep gullies. Over the years, the ridges were partially covered with trees and other vegetation. Today there are more than 2,842 acres in the park, along with 22 ponds. In 1986, the Middle Fork River became Illinois's first scenic river. In 1989, it was designated as a National Scenic River by the U.S. Secretary of the Interior. The river is now protected by state and federal law because of its outstanding scenic, recreational, ecological, and historical importance. The Mountain Bike Trail at Kickapoo State Park consists of five loop segments totaling over 6 miles. These excellent trails were developed by the Kickapoo Mountain Bike Club

Lake along loop 4, Kickapoo State Park

with the help of park staff. To reach the trailhead, bikers can park by the main office and ride past the road toward Emerald Pond and Inland Sea or park at a small parking area at the turn to go to Emerald Pond. Just past this road, and the trailhead to the Out and Back Hiking Trail, is a large wooden sign that marks the Mountain Bike Trail. The trail is marked with metal markers that have a symbol of a bicycle on them and an arrow pointing the direction of travel.

The mountain bike trail joins the horse trail at times and then splits off. It also crosses the Out and Back Hiking Trail numerous times; no bicycle riding is allowed on the horse trail or the Out and Back Trail. At times the horse trail splits off and horses are banned from certain segments of the mountain bike trail. Parts of the trails are recommended to be traveled in one direction and are signed by direction arrows. In addition to the main trailhead, two other trailheads are located in the park. Bikers can get to the second trailhead by taking Kickapoo Park Road to 1200 E and parking in the Public Hunting Area parking lot. The third trailhead is found by taking 1200 E to 2000 N. Turn west at

Sign on trail, Kickapoo State Park

2000 N, then north on 1180 E. Turn west on 2030 N and proceed to the end of this road to the small parking area.

The first trail segment goes through some wooded areas on a winding level route. It comes out to a large prairie and then heads toward the edge of a tree line. The trail is joined here with the return loop and the horse trail. The trail then goes north and east, passing by a spoil pile and a small wetland, and then comes to an old gravel road. Head east on this road to the second trailhead and parking area at 1200 E and Kickapoo Road. Prior to reaching the parking area, the trail will head into the woods for a short distance. The trail heads west, then north and west again, going by a prairie parallel to the road. The trail then goes up a small hill, goes through a nice wooded area, and comes back out to the gravel road again. The trail goes northwest along the gravel road for a short distance until the third loop is reached.

The third loop is a short loop that goes through some woods and around a prairie. It soon joins with the fourth loop. The fourth loop is a scenic loop with some nicely wooded areas. It goes around a prairie, down a steep grade, along a ridge, and then descends a steep hill. Halfway through the fourth loop is the fifth.

The fifth loop is a single-lane trail marked in orange arrows spray-painted on the trees. This is the newest loop segment. It is a relatively level trail except for two steep ravines. The first part of the trail follows the perimeter of the deep ravine on your left. Halfway through the trail, it comes to the edge of a hill overlooking a pond with the gravel road in the background. Beyond the pond, the trail winds around wooded areas and a prairie, connecting with the fourth loop again. Prior to descending the hill at the end of the fourth loop, you will see a large strip-mined lake to the right. Part of the descent is washed out, so you must be cautious. This area is a scenic spot to take a break and rest. From here, a short segment of the trail goes to the right of the gravel road, following a ridge for a quarter mile. The trail connects with the gravel road and soon goes by small bluffs and the pond seen from the fifth loop. The other trail loops cross this road, and soon a leg for the first loop comes up to the right. Take the second half of loop one back, passing by the group camping area, back to the trailhead.

Additions are planned for this trail in the future. Mountain bike races are held here occasionally.

Facilities: There are numerous picnic areas in the park with tables, water, grills, toilets, and playground equipment. A concession stand offers refreshments as well as canoe and boat rentals. Call to check on the river conditions before coming out to canoe. Camping is available. Boat launch ramps are provided on nine lakes. Scuba diving is allowed in Inland Sea and Sportsman's Lake, with prior registration with park staff. A fishing license is required to fish the lakes and the Vermilion River.

Park Rules and Regulations: Watch for hikers and horseback riders. Ride only on the designated mountain bike trail. Keep to right. Foot traffic yields to bikes. Obey all signs. Stay off trails during wet and muddy conditions. No swimming. No riding during the deer hunting season.

Hours Open: The park opens at 8:00 A.M. and closes at 10:00 P.M., except for campers and fishermen.

Mailing Address and Phone Number: Kickapoo State Park, 10906 Kickapoo Park Road, Oakwood, IL 61858; 217-442-4915, or Kickapoo Mountain Bike Club, P.O. Box 475, Oakwood, IL 61858

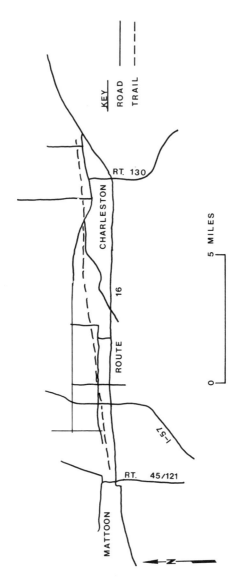

Charleston-Mattoon Bike Trail. Redrawn from Illinois Department of Transportation County Highway map.

43. Charleston-Mattoon Bike Trail (under construction)

Trail Length: 12 miles, one way

Trail Surface: Limestone screenings, asphalt

County: Coles

Location: The Charleston-Mattoon Bike Trail is a rail-trail between the eastern side of Mattoon and the eastern side of Charleston. To reach Mattoon, travelers can take I-57 to Route 16 (exit 190). Head west into Mattoon. Travelers to Charleston can take Route 16 east into Charleston.

Trail Description: The proposed Charleston-Mattoon Bike Trail was in the final engineering stages in 1996. When completed, the trail will link the two communities. Currently there is a small portion of trail in each city that may be used.

Facilities: Numerous parks and establishments are found in Mattoon and Charleston.

Park Rules and Regulations: No unauthorized motor vehicles allowed.

Hours Open: To be announced

Mailing Address and Phone Number: City of Charleston, 520 Jackson Ave., Charleston, IL 61920; 217-345-5650

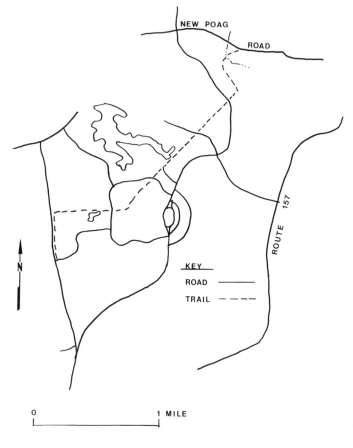

NEW POAG
ROAD

ROUTE 157

KEY
ROAD ———
TRAIL -----

0   1 MILE

Delyte W. Morris Bicycle Trail

44. Delyte W. Morris Bicycle Trail

Trail Length: 3 miles, one way

Trail Surface: Dirt, limestone, asphalt

County: Madison

Location: The Delyte W. Morris Bicycle Trail is found on the campus of Southern Illinois University in Edwardsville. To reach the trail, take State Route 157 and head west out of Edwardsville toward campus. In a few miles turn north at University Drive. Turn west at the traffic signals. Proceed for a short distance until you see a sign for the Tower Lake Recreation Area.

Trail Description: The trail at the parking area is an asphalt trail that goes both northeast and southwest from

Pedestrian bridge over trail, Delyte W. Morris Bicycle Trail

Delyte W. Morris Bicycle Trail

Creek crossing, Delyte W. Morris Bicycle Trail

the Tower Lake Recreation Area. Traveling northeast, it soon passes by Tower Lake and goes under two roads before the surface becomes dirt. The trail then winds through a small wooded stream valley, over a wooden bridge, and out of the valley, ending at New Poag Road. Bikers can continue riding along Poag Road east into Edwardsville or west down into the wide open American Bottoms, the lowlands of the Mississippi River.

Heading south from the Tower Lake parking lot, one goes through campus, under Campus Drive, and under a small pedestrian bridge and then again under Campus Drive where the trail turns to limestone screenings. The trail goes by a small wooded area and a pond. It continues south and goes over a wooden bridge and by a small parking area located on Bluff Road. The trail then parallels Bluff Road south for a short distance and ends at Whiteside Road. Directly across the street is a soccer complex where bathrooms and a parking area are located.

Facilities: Facilities are found on campus.

Delyte W. Morris Bicycle Trail

Rules and Regulations: None posted

Hours Open: None posted

Mailing Address and Phone Number: Campus Recreation, Southern Illinois University at Edwardsville, P.O. Box 1157, Edwardsville, IL 62026; 618-692-3235

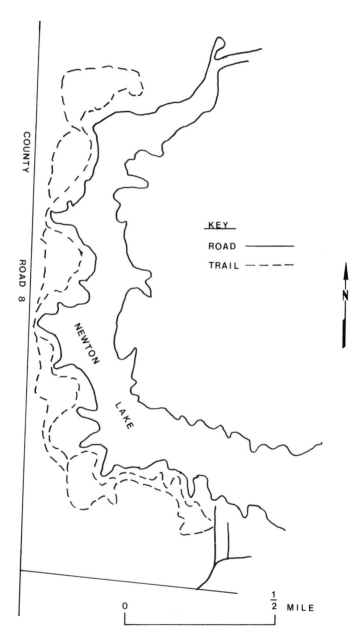

KEY

ROAD ——————

TRAIL — — — —

N

COUNTY

ROAD 8

NEWTON

LAKE

0 $\frac{1}{2}$ MILE

Newton Lake State Fish and Wildlife Area

45. Newton Lake State Fish and Wildlife Area

Trail Length: 4.6 miles

Trail Surface: Dirt, grass

County: Jasper

Location: Newton Lake Conservation Area is located on the west side of Newton Lake. The park is located 10 miles southwest of the town of Newton and 25 miles southeast of Effingham. To reach the park, take State Route 33 out of Effingham. Fifteen miles out of Effingham there is a sign to turn south on County Road 8, known as 500 E. Proceed on this road to 700 E and head west, then south on 300 E following the signs to the park entrance, in 10 miles.

Trail Description: Newton Lake was impounded by the Central Illinois Public Service Company (CIPS) to provide water for its Newton electric power generating plant. In 1979, the Illinois Department of Conservation, now the Illinois Department of Natural Resources, signed a one-year lease with CIPS that designates the 1,755-acre Newton Lake and 540 acres of shoreland as a day-use conservation area. By agreement, recreational activities in the area consist of bank and boat fishing, picnicking, hiking, and horseback riding. CIPS financed the initial recreational development of the area. In 1996 park staff constructed a 4.6-mile mountain bike trail that begins north of the park office and heads north, paralleling the west side of the lake and going through some nice wooded areas and open fields and by the edge of a farm field.

Signs of ongoing work on this new trail, such as small tree stumps, and other work, for example, cul-

Trailboard, Newton Lake State Fish and Wildlife Area

verts being installed, can be seen along the route. In addition, there are a few steep trail segments to descend and climb.

There is a trailboard just north of the park office. A trail map and rules are posted there. The trail is marked with metal bike signs as well as orange and red streamers on trees. Currently, there are four trail loops that total 4.6 miles. The trails are either dirt through the wooded portions or wide grass lanes on the return loops. The trails are set up to travel in one direction: counterclockwise on the loops.

The first trail segment comes down to the lake and runs parallel to it for a short distance. Views of the lake are good, especially when the trees are bare. The trail comes out to an open field and goes under some power lines (twice), over a bridge, and then back into the woods. At a small pond near the road is a picnic table. A connecting trail leads toward the park road and the return loop. From the pond, the trail heads into the woods and then toward the road where a steep grade

Trail marker, Newton Lake State Fish and Wildlife Area

is encountered. The trail parallels the road, goes over a small wooden bridge, and climbs uphill. A good vantage point of the lake is found here. This is a small loop, and it connects with another small loop. The third loop also is on a hill and goes around the ravines. It soon connects with the fourth loop, which is in a nice wooded section with some views of the lake. There are some handsome old oak trees in this segment. The trail winds its way around a hill, passing by some scenic ravines, and soon connects with the third loop. From here, one can take the return half of the loops back to the trailhead. The return loops stay in an open grassy environment for the most part, heading into the woods only a few times, and the last return loop parallels a farm field for a short time.

For future trail extensions, contact the park for additional information.

Facilities: A site office is located in the park to provide information. Picnic facilities are located at the north and south access areas. A boat ramp is located at the south access area. Currently, there are no concessions or rental services available at the site. Water is available at the site office, and toilets are located by the parking area. There are no camping facilities at Newton Lake; primitive camping may be found at Sam Parr State Park 16 miles from the lake, and there is a private campground about 4 miles south of the dam. Fishing is allowed in Newton Lake with all Illinois fishing rules and regulations in effect.

Park Rules and Regulations: No horses or all terrain vehicles allowed on the mountain bike trail. No littering. No bikes allowed on the hiking and horse trail. Swimming, camping, ice fishing, and hunting are prohibited.

Hours Open: The park is open every day of the year except Christmas Day and New Year's Day. The park closes at 10:00 P.M. daily.

Mailing Address and Phone Number: Newton Lake State Fish and Wildlife Area, 3490 E. 500th Ave., Newton, IL 62448; 618-783-3478

46. Red Hills State Park

Trail Length: 5 miles

Trail Surface: Dirt, grass

County: Lawrence

Location: Red Hills State Park is located east of Olney. To reach the park, take Route 250 out of Olney east for 2 miles to State Route 50. Continue heading east on Route 50 for 12 miles to the park entrance. There is a sign along the road for the park, with the main entrance to the park found on the south side of Route 50. The south park entrance may also be reached by taking State Route 250 through Sumner to the south entrance.

Trail Description: The mountain bike trail at Red Hills State Park is the shared horse trail. The trailhead is found at the south end of the park off Route 250. Travelers on Route 50 may come in at the north entrance, and drive through the park, or park at a few locations in the park to get on the trail. The trail goes in a counterclockwise direction, and there are trail markers with a horse symbol, hiker, or a bicycle. The trail does a loop around the park lake and goes through wooded areas, stream valleys, and uplands. It varies from a wide dirt trail to a single lane trail. Below the dam, a steep hill leading to the creek valley will be encountered. The trailhead is found at the south end of the park and on the east side of the road, as one enters from Route 250. A small parking area is found here along with a horse sign. On the other side of the road is the horse campground. The trail then goes by an open field that has wildlife food plots and a wildlife viewing stand. The trail goes through some open fields winding around the fields. Keep your eyes open for the trail markers in this

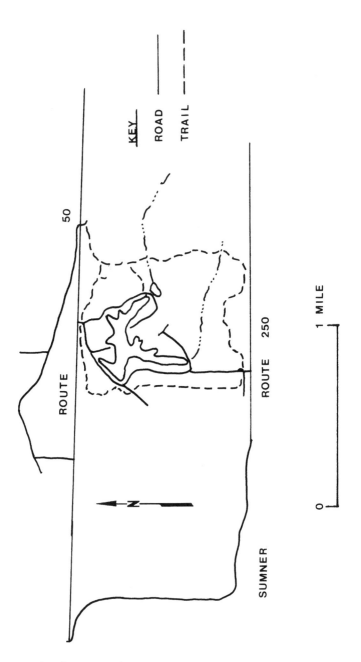

KEY

ROAD ──────

TRAIL ── ── ──

50

ROUTE

ROUTE 250

N

0 1 MILE

SUMNER

Red Hills State Park

area since it is a little confusing and there are other trails, but few trail markers.

The trail goes through some small wooded areas and by a small parking lot off Route 250. From here, the trail makes its way to a ridge where there are open fields on a ridgetop. It goes through some of these fields and then joins a connecting trail. This trail heads west and connects back with the park road. The trail then heads down a hill, goes through a wooded area, and comes across a trail junction to the right. This trail parallels Route 50 and comes out across from the north area entrance. It then parallels Route 50, goes up and down a few small hills, and comes out at the park entrance, crossing the road. The trail continues through a wooded area as a single-lane trail heading west and paralleling Route 50. It makes its way downhill and finally drops down to the creek valley below the dam. This creek must be forded, and on the other side is a steep hill.

Past the dam, the trail comes out to the park road, via a connecting trail, soon passes the ranger's house, and parallels a tree line and old airplane landing field. The trail goes by a small pond and then comes out at the horse camping area and the trailhead.

Facilities: A lake is found here along with a restaurant on the lake's edge. Campgrounds are available, as well as picnic areas, water, restrooms, playground equipment, additional hiking trails, and a boat launch. Hunting is also allowed in the park.

Park Rules and Regulations: Pets must be on a leash.

Hours Open: The park closes at 10:00 P.M.

Mailing Address and Phone Number: Red Hills State Park, R.R. 2, Box 252A, Sumner, IL 62466, 618-936-2469

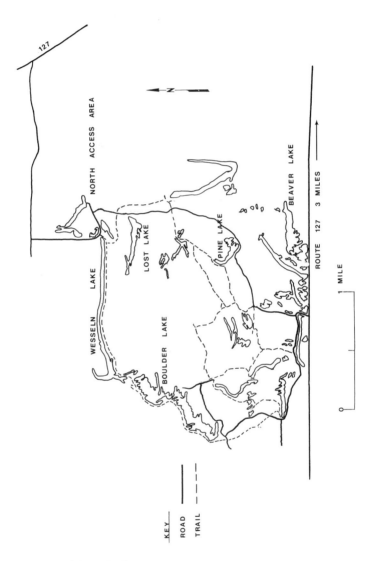

KEY

ROAD

TRAIL

Pyramid State Park

127

NORTH ACCESS AREA

N

WESSELN LAKE

LOST LAKE

BOULDER LAKE

PINE LAKE

BEAVER LAKE

ROUTE 127

3 MILES

0   1 MILE

47. Pyramid State Park

Trail Length: 12 miles

Trail Surface: Dirt, rock

County: Perry

Location: Pyramid State Park is located 6 miles south-west of Pinckneyville. To reach the main park entrance, north and south traffic may take State Route 127. A sign for the park is located 3 miles south of Pinckneyville. Turn west on this road and go approximately 3 miles to the park entrance. Trails may also be reached from the north access area. To get to the north access area, go 2 miles north of the park road on Route 127 to a gravel road. Turn west on this road, go over a set of railroad tracks, pass by a coal company building, and proceed for a mile and a half to the park entrance. There is a sign along the road indicating Pyramid State Park, North Area.

Trail Description: Pyramid State Park gets its name from one of the major coal companies in Perry County that was strip-mining land in this area. The park was formerly used as Southern Illinois University's Research Area. In 1965, the State of Illinois acquired 1,600 acres of land and has since increased the acreage to over 2,528 acres. The park features rough topography with multiple ridges and cuts that resulted from mining operations between 1930 and 1950. Numerous lakes and ponds were created by the strip-mining operation; they vary in size up to 24 acres and total more than 135 acres of water. The park is now heavily wooded with cotton-wood, box elder, sycamore, small oak, and hickory trees.

The trail system in the park consists of multipurpose trails shared by bikers, hikers, and horseback rid-

Trailboard, Pyramid State Park

ers. Mountain bike riders may ride on the same trails as the horse riders; some trails are open only to hikers. The trail system may be started west of the park office or north of the office where parking is available.

The trail is about 8 feet wide and generally follows mine spoil ridge tops. It offers some beautiful views of the numerous small ponds and lakes in the park. The trails in the center of the park are all well marked with wooden posts bearing the name and direction of the trail. Horse or hiker symbols are also seen along the trails.

If you start riding the trail north of the office, you can do a loop around the center of the park, going by some hike and bike campgrounds and the Chain of Lakes. Heading east, you will join another trail that takes you by Pine Lake. Past Pine Lake is a loop trail that will take the rider back to the center of the park toward the Chain of Lakes, or one can continue east.

Hike/bike campsite, Pyramid State Park

From the Chain of Lakes, one can ride north around some small lakes and head toward the horse camping area.

Shortly after the intersection, the trail passes Blackberry Lake and goes over the park road toward Beehive Lake, which is at the north park access. A side trail off the main trail leads to Beehive Lake. Lost Lake is to the south, and a connecting trail for hiking only takes you to this lake. Continuing west, you will soon see Wesseln Lake from the north side of the trail. The trail parallels this lake for about a mile and a half. The trail then goes between Boulder Lake and Wesseln Lake, paralleling the west side of Boulder Lake. Close to the south end of Boulder Lake, the trail crosses the park road and goes by Pine Grove Picnic Area. A shelter, picnic tables, and restrooms are available here. Beyond Pine Grove Picnic Area, the trail passes by an open field and wooded area going toward Heron Lake. Between Heron Lake and Marsh Lake the trail is fun riding, going up and down the rugged terrain. The rider goes past Marsh Lake and to the horse campground. From here, a trail east goes toward Hidden Lake passing by some camping areas, and another trail south goes past Hook Lake. A connecting trail takes the rider toward Chain of Lakes, where the trails in the center of the park are.

There are numerous hike and bike campsites available in the center of the park. These campsites have picnic tables, garbage cans, and an area for a fire. Permits are required to camp here. If the park office is closed, fill out a permit form, put your car license on the permit and a general indication of where you are camping, and drop the permit in the drop box at the office.

Facilities: A park office located in the park has additional information. Many picnic areas, which have tables, restrooms, and stoves, are scattered through the park. More than a hundred tent and trailer campsites are in the park. Water is available at the park office. There are also boat launches on the larger lakes. Fishing is allowed on any of the lakes in the park, contingent upon all Illinois fishing rules and regulations. Horse trail parking is located west of the park office. Restrooms, picnic tables, grills, a boat launch, and camping facilities are available at the north access area.

Park Rules and Regulations: The bike trail is closed October 15 to April 15, annually. In addition, the trails will be closed during heavy rains. No vehicles on the trails. Horse camping area is restricted to horse campers only. Horses must stay on the trails and are not permitted on or along roads, except where the trail crosses the park road. Camping is permitted only in designated areas. Ten is the maximum horsepower on the lakes. Swimming, diving, and bathing are prohibited. No fires are permitted on the ground.

Hours Open: The park is open all year except on Christmas Day and New Year's Day. At certain times, because of freezing and thawing periods, the park is closed, and access to the park is by foot only. The park closes at 10:00 P.M. except for campers.

Mailing Address and Phone Number: Pyramid State Park, R.R. 1, Box 290, Pinckneyville, IL 62274; 618-357-2574

48. Tunnel Hill State Trail (under construction)

Trail Length: 44.5 miles, one way

Trail Surface: Limestone screenings, asphalt

Counties: Saline, Williamson, Johnson, and Pulaski

Location: The Tunnel Hill State Trail is located in southern Illinois and will go from Harrisburg to Karnak. Travelers to Harrisburg can take Route 13 into Harrisburg and turn south on Route 45 to go to the trailhead. To reach the southern end of the trail in Karnak, travelers can take Route 45 south out of Harrisburg to Route 169. Turn west on Route 169 and proceed into Karnak.

Trail Description: The final engineering plans were being prepared for the Tunnel Hill State Trail in 1996. The proposed rail-trail along the Norfolk-Southern Railroad stretches from Harrisburg to Karnak for a distance of 44.5 miles. The State of Illinois owns 42 miles and the City of Harrisburg owns the northern 2.5 miles. This trail will be one of the most beautiful trails in the state when completed, as it passes through the heart of the Shawnee National Forest.

According to Molie Oliver, site superintendent for Tunnel Hill State Trail, "the trail goes through coal mine and farming areas, as well as beautiful natural areas, including the Cache River Natural Area. The Little Cache and Sugar Creeks will also be crossed. Elevation will go from 350 feet to 700 feet with beautiful rock outcrops, bluffs, and ravines." As the name suggests, the trail will also go through an abandoned tunnel built in 1929, at 550 feet in length, south of Tunnel Hill. "The trail will also go over 21 trestles which range from 35

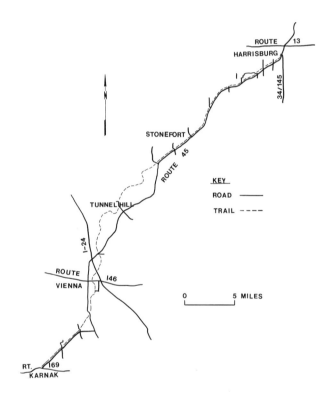

Tunnel Hill State Trail. Redrawn from Illinois Department of
Transportation maps.

Tunnel Hill State Trail

to 430 feet in length, and will pass through nine communities. The trail is being developed in sections; the section between Vienna and Tunnel Hill being developed first (10 miles)." The Harrisburg section is currently open for use.

Facilities: The site office and visitor center will be located in Vienna. Restaurants and service stations are found in Harrisburg, Carrier Mills, and Vienna. Parking facilities will be found in eight communities along the trail.

Park Rules and Regulations: No motorized vehicles or hunting.

Hours Open: To be announced.

Mailing Address and Phone Number: Tunnel Hill State Trail, P.O. Box 10, Goreville, IL 62939; 618-995-2177

Appendixes
Selected Bibliography

Mountain Bike Clubs in Illinois

Bicycle Club of Lake County*
P.O. Box 521
Libertyville, IL 60048

Folks on Spokes*
P.O. Box 824
Homewood, IL 60430

Trail Users Rights Foundation (TURF)*
P.O. Box 403
Summit, IL 60501

RIDE, Inc.*
208 S. La Salle, Suite 1700
Chicago, IL 60604

Blackhawk Bicycle and Ski Club*
P.O. Box 6443
Rockford, IL 61125

Kickapoo Mountain Bike Club
P.O. Box 61850
Oakwood, IL 61850

Peoria Bicycle Club*
1406 Fayette Ave.
Washington, IL 61571

Shawnee Mountain Bike Association
190 Battleford Road
Harrisburg, IL 62946

*International Mountain Bike Association Club Affiliate

Appendix B

Trail Organizations

Chicagoland Bicycle Federation
417 S. Dearborn, Room 1000
Chicago, IL 60605-1120
(312) 427-3325

Friends of the Illinois and Michigan Canal National
Heritage Corridor
19 W. 580 83d Street
Downers Grove, IL 60516

Friends of the Rock Island Trail
P.O. Box 272
Peoria, IL 61650

Gateway Trailnet
7185 Manchester Road
St. Louis, MO 63143
(618) 874-8554

Illinois Prairie Path
P.O. Box 1086
Wheaton, IL 60189
(630) 752-0120

League of Illinois Bicyclists
417 S. Dearborn, Room 1000
Chicago, IL 60605-1120
(708) 481-3429

Rails-to-Trails Conservancy, Illinois Chapter
319 W. Cook Street
Springfield, IL 62704
(217) 789-4782

Where to Order Maps for Illinois

The U.S.G.S. publishes a series of standard topographical maps for Illinois. The unit of survey is a quadrangle bounded by parallels of latitude and meridians of longitude. U.S.G.S. topographic maps may be ordered from:

U.S. Geological Survey
Earth Science Information Center
1400 Independence Rd.
Rolla, MO 65401
(573) 341-0851

or:

U.S. Geological Survey, Map Sales
Box 25286, Federal Center
Denver, CO 80225
(800) 435-7627

Topographical maps for Illinois may also be ordered from the Illinois State Geological Survey at:

Illinois State Geological Survey
Natural Resources Building
615 E. Peabody Drive
Champaign, IL 61820
(217) 333-4747

Maps may also be purchased at selected sporting or camping goods stores throughout the state.

The Illinois Department of Transportation (IDOT) prepares and publishes various special-purpose state, county, township, and city maps that are available for sale to the general public. A description of the maps available for Illinois and their prices may be obtained from IDOT at the following address:

Map Sales, Room 121
Illinois Department of Transportation
2300 Dirksen Parkway
Springfield, IL 62764
(217) 782-0834

Topographic maps for the Shawnee National Forest may be obtained by contacting one of the following Forest Service offices:

Forest Supervisor
Shawnee National Forest
Harrisburg, IL 62946
(800) 699-6637

District Ranger
Shawnee National Forest
Elizabethtown, IL 62946
(618) 287-2201

District Ranger
Shawnee National Forest
Jonesboro, IL 62952
(618) 833-8576

District Ranger
Shawnee National Forest
Murphysboro, IL 62966
(618) 687-1731

District Ranger
Shawnee National Forest
Vienna, IL 62995
(618) 658-2111

International Mountain Bicycling Association Rules of the Trail

Thousands of miles of dirt trails have been closed to mountain bicyclists. The irresponsible riding habits of a few riders have been a factor. Do your part to maintain trail access by observing the following rules of the trail, formulated by the International Mountain Bicycling Association (IMBA). IMBA's mission is to promote environmentally sound and socially responsible mountain biking.

1. Ride on open trails only. Respect trail and road closures (ask if not sure), avoid possible trespass on private land, obtain permits and authorization as may be required. Federal and state wilderness areas are closed to cycling. The way you ride will influence trail management decisions and policies.

2. Leave no trace. Be sensitive to the dirt beneath you. Even on open (legal) trails, you should not ride under conditions where you will leave evidence of your passing, such as on certain soils after a rain. Recognize different types of soils and trail construction; practice low-impact cycling. This also means staying on existing trails and not creating any new ones. Be sure to pack out at least as much as you pack in.

3. Control your bicycle! Inattention for even a second can cause problems. Obey all bicycle speed regulations and recommendations.

4. Always yield trail. Make known your approach well in advance. A friendly greeting (or bell) is considerate and works well; don't startle others. Show your respect when passing by slowing to a walking pace or even

Source: International Mountain Bicycling Association, Rules of the Trail

stopping. Anticipate other trail users around corners or in blind spots.

5. Never spook animals. All animals are startled by an unannounced approach, a sudden movement, or a loud noise. This can be dangerous for you, others, and the animals. Give animals extra room and time to adjust to you. When passing horses use special care and follow directions from the horseback riders (ask if uncertain). Running cattle and disturbing wildlife is a serious offense. Leave gates as you found them, or as marked.

6. Plan ahead. Know your equipment, your ability, and the area in which you are riding—and prepare accordingly. Be self-sufficient at all times, keep your equipment in good repair, and carry necessary supplies for changes in weather or other conditions. A well-executed trip is a satisfaction to you and not a burden or offense to others. Always wear a helmet.

Keep trails open by setting a good example of environmentally sound and socially responsible off-road cycling.

Appendix E
Bicycle Rules of the Road

Article XV. Bicycles

5/11-1501. Application of rules
11-1501. Application of rules. (a) It is unlawful for any person to do any act forbidden or fail to perform any act required in Article XV of Chapter 11 of this Code. (b) The parent of any child and the guardian of any ward shall not authorize or knowingly permit any such child or ward to violate any of the provisions of this Code.

5/11-1502. Traffic laws apply to persons riding bicycles
11-1502. Traffic laws apply to persons riding bicycles. Every person riding a bicycle upon a highway shall be granted all of the rights and shall be subject to all of the duties applicable to the driver of a vehicle by this Code, except as to special regulations in this Article XV and except as to those provisions of this Code which by their nature can have no application.

5/11-1503. Riding on bicycles
11-1503. Riding on bicycles. (a) A person propelling a bicycle shall not ride other than upon or astride a permanent and regular seat attached thereto. (b) No bicycle shall be used to carry more persons at one time than the number for which it is designed and equipped, except that an adult rider may carry a child securely attached to his person in a back pack or sling.

5/11-1504. Clinging to vehicles
11-1504. Clinging to vehicles. No person riding upon any bicycle, coaster, roller skates, sled or toy vehicle

Source: Illinois Motor Vehicle Code, Illinois Compiled Statutes, 1994.

shall attach the same or himself to any vehicle upon a roadway.

5/11-1505. Position of bicycles and motorized pedal cycles on roadways—Riding on roadways and bicycle paths

11-1505. Position of bicycles and motorized pedal cycles on roadways—Riding on roadways and bicycle paths.

(a) Any person operating a bicycle or motorized pedal cycle upon a roadway at less than the normal speed of traffic at the time and place and under the conditions then existing shall ride as close as practicable to the right-hand curb or edge of the roadway except under the following situations:

1. When overtaking and passing another bicycle, motorized pedal cycle or vehicle proceeding in the same direction;

2. When preparing for a left turn at an intersection or into a private road or driveway; or

3. When reasonably necessary to avoid conditions including, but not limited to, fixed or moving objects, parked or moving vehicles, bicycles, motorized pedal cycles, pedestrians, animals, surface hazards, or substandard width lanes that make it unsafe to continue along the right-hand curb or edge. For purposes of this subsection, a "substandard width lane" means a lane that is too narrow for a bicycle or motorized pedal cycle and a vehicle to travel safely side by side within the lane.

(b) Any person operating a bicycle or motorized pedal cycle upon a one-way highway with two or more marked traffic lanes may ride as near the left-hand curb or edge of such roadway as practicable.

5/11-1505.1. Riding bicycles or motorized pedal cycles on roadways

11-1505.1. Persons riding bicycles or motorized pedal cycles upon a roadway shall not ride more than 2 abreast, except on paths or parts of roadways set aside for their exclusive use. Persons riding 2 abreast shall not impede the normal and reasonable movement of traffic and, on a laned roadway, shall ride within a single lane subject to the provisions of Section 11-1505.

5/11-1506. Carrying articles

11–1506. Carrying articles. No person operating a bicycle shall carry any package, bundle or article which prevents the use of both hands in the control and operation of the bicycle. A person operating a bicycle shall keep at least one hand on the handle bars at all times.

5/11-1507. Lamps and other equipment on bicycles

11-1507. Lamps and other equipment on bicycles. (a) Every bicycle when in use at night time shall be equipped with a lamp on the front which shall emit a white light visible from a distance of at least 500 feet to the front and with a red reflector on the rear of a type approved by the Department which shall be visible from all distances from 100 feet to 600 feet to the rear when directly in front of lawful lower beams of head lamps on a motor vehicle. A lamp emitting a red light visible from a distance of 500 feet to the rear may be used in addition to the red reflector. (b) A bicycle shall not be equipped with nor shall any person use upon a bicycle any siren. (c) Every bicycle shall be equipped with a brake which will adequately control movement of and stop and hold such bicycle. (d) No person shall sell a new bicycle or pedal for use on a bicycle that is not equipped with a reflex reflector conforming to specifications prescribed by the Department, on each pedal, visible from the front and rear of the bicycle during darkness from a distance of 200 feet. (e) No person shall sell or offer for sale a new bicycle that is not equipped with side reflectors. Such reflectors shall be visible from each side of the bicycle from a distance of 500 feet and shall be essentially colorless or red to the rear of the center of the bicycle and essentially colorless or amber to the front of the center of the bicycle provided. The requirements of this paragraph may be met by reflective materials which shall be at least 3/16 of an inch wide on each side of each tire or rim to indicate as clearly as possible the continuous circular shape and size of the tires or rims of such bicycle and which reflective materials may be of the same color on both the front and rear tire or rim. Such reflectors shall conform to specifications prescribed by the Department. (f) No person shall sell or offer for sale a new bicycle that is not equipped with an essentially colorless front-facing reflector.

5/11-1507.1. Lamps on motorized pedal cycles
11-1507.1. Lamps on motorized pedal cycles. Every motorized pedal cycle, when in use at night time, shall be equipped with a lamp on the front which shall emit a white light visible from a distance of at least 500 feet to the front, and with a red reflector on the rear of a type approved by the Department which shall be visible from all distances from 100 feet to 600 feet to the rear when in front of lawful, low-powered beams of head lamps on a motor vehicle. A lamp emitting a red light visible from a distance of 500 feet to the rear may be used in addition to the red reflector.

5/11-1508. Bicycle identifying number
11-1508. Bicycle identifying number. A person engaged in the business of selling bicycles at retail shall not sell any bicycle unless the bicycle has an identifying number permanently stamped or cast on its frame.

5/11-1509. Inspecting bicycles
11-1509. Inspecting bicycles. A uniformed police officer may at any time upon reasonable cause to believe that a bicycle is unsafe or not equipped as required by law, or that its equipment is not in proper adjustment or repair, require the person riding the bicycle to stop and submit the bicycle to an inspection and such test with reference thereto as may be appropriate.

5/11-1510. Left turns
11-1510. Left Turns. (a) A person riding a bicycle or motorized pedal cycle intending to turn left shall follow a course described in Section 11–801 or in paragraph (b) of this Section. (b) A person riding a bicycle or motorized pedal cycle intending to turn left shall approach the turn as close as practicable to the right curb or edge

of the roadway. After proceeding across the intersecting roadway to the far corner of the curb or intersection of the roadway edges, the bicyclist or motorized pedal cycle driver shall stop, as much as practicable out of the way of traffic. After stopping the person shall yield to any traffic proceeding in either direction along the roadway such person had been using. After yielding, the bicycle or motorized pedal cycle driver shall comply with any official traffic control device or police officer regulating traffic on the highway along which he intends to proceed, and the bicyclist or motorized pedal cycle driver may proceed in the new direction. (c) Notwithstanding the foregoing provisions, the Department and local authorities in their respective jurisdictions may cause official traffic-control devices to be placed and thereby require and direct that a specific course be traveled by turning bicycles and motorized pedal cycles, and when such devices are so placed, no person shall turn a bicycle or motorized pedal cycle other than as directed and required by such devices.

5/11-1511. Turn and stop signals

11-1511. Turn and stop signals. (a) Except as provided in this Section, a person riding a bicycle shall comply with Section 11-804. (b) A signal of intention to turn right or left when required shall be given during not less than the last 100 feet traveled by the bicycle before turning, and shall be given while the bicycle is stopped waiting to turn. A signal by hand and arm need not be given continuously if the hand is needed in the control or operation of the bicycle.

5/11-1512. Bicycles on sidewalks

11-1512. Bicycles on sidewalks. (a) A person propelling a bicycle upon and along a sidewalk, or across a roadway upon and along a crosswalk, shall yield the right of way to any pedestrian and shall give audible signal before overtaking and passing such pedestrian. (b) A person shall not ride a bicycle upon and along a sidewalk, or across a roadway upon and along a crosswalk, where such use of bicycles is prohibited by official traffic-control devices.

(c) A person propelling a bicycle upon and along a sidewalk or across a roadway upon and along a crosswalk, shall have all the rights and duties applicable to a pedestrian under the same circumstances.

5/11-1513. Bicycle parking
11-1513. Bicycle parking. (a) A person may park a bicycle on a sidewalk unless prohibited or restricted by an official traffic-control device. (b) A bicycle parked on a sidewalk shall not impede the normal and reasonable movement of pedestrian or other traffic. (c) A bicycle may be parked on the roadway at any angle to the curb or edge of the roadway at any location where parking is allowed. (d) A bicycle may be parked on the roadway abreast of another bicycle or bicycles near the side of the roadway at any location where parking is allowed. (e) A person shall not park a bicycle on a roadway in such a manner as to obstruct the movement of a legally parked motor vehicle. (f) In all other respects, bicycles parked anywhere on a highway shall conform with the provisions of this Code regulating the parking of vehicles.

5/11-1514. Bicycle racing
11-1514. Bicycle racing. (a) Bicycle racing on a highway shall not be unlawful when a racing event has been approved by State or local authorities on any highway under their respective jurisdictions. Approval of bicycle highway racing events shall be granted only under conditions which assure reasonable safety for all race participants, spectators and other highway users, and which prevent unreasonable interference with traffic flow which would seriously inconvenience other highway users. (b) By agreement with the approving authority, participants, in an approved bicycle highway racing event may be exempted from compliance with any traffic laws otherwise applicable thereto, provided that traffic control is adequate to assure the safety of all highway users.

5/11-1515. Operation of a commercial bicycle messenger service; insurance coverage
11-1515. No person, firm, or corporation shall operate

a commercial bicycle messenger service in a city with a population of more than 2,000,000 unless the bicycles used are covered by a liability insurance policy at the expense of the person, firm, or corporation. The insurance policy shall be issued in amounts no less than the minimum amounts set for bodily injury or death and for destruction of property under Section 7-203 of this Code. No insurer other than an insurer authorized to do business in this State shall issue a policy under this Section.

The Grand Illinois Trail

The Grand Illinois Trail is a 475 mile loop trail proposed for northern Illinois. This trail concept was developed by the Illinois Department of Natural Resources (DNR) and supported by the Rails-to-Trails Conservancy, Illinois Chapter. The trail begins or ends in the Chicagoland area and circles northern Illinois toward Rockford, Freeport, Galena, Quad Cities, along the Hennepin and Illinois and Michigan Canals, and the Illinois Prairie Path, as well as on other trails and through other communities.

The DNR's goal is to have one continuous linking trail by the year 2000. Currently, over 150 miles of trail (over 20 different trails), are in place. The trails are managed by various state and local government and nonprofit organizations. Where there are gaps between trail segments, local roads may be used to get to the next trail stretch.

A main goal of this trail concept is to bring together all of the trails as one link to provide a long-distance trail system. A second goal is link the trails so travelers can travel from Lake Michigan to the Mississippi River and back.

In 1996, Mike Ulm and Kandee Hartel of the Rails-to-Trails, Illinois Chapter, biked, hiked, canoed, roller bladed and rode horseback the entire proposed trail network. Their trip, referred to as the "Grand Illinois Adventure," was completed in three weeks, ending on National Trails Day (June 1). This marked the first time that this Grand Illinois Trail Segment was completed in its entirety. The main purpose of this trip was to promote this trail concept as they traveled through all the cities on the trail network. Walter Zyznieuski helped draft a proposed routing of this adventure for Rails-to-Trails.

The trails that comprise this network are still being put together. The trail surfaces for the existing trails are asphalt, dirt, grass, limestone screenings, and roadways. The trails that mountain bike riders would be most interested in riding include the Hennepin and Illinois and Michigan Canals, the Illinois Prairie Path, the Pecatonica Prairie Path, and the Des Plaines River Trails–Cook and Lake Counties.

For additional information on the Grand Illinois Trail, you may contact the Rails-to-Trails office listed in Appendix B or the Illinois Department of Natural Resources at:

Division of Planning
Illinois Department of Natural Resources
524 S. 2d St.
Springfield, IL 62701-1787

Selected Bibliography

Davis, Don, and Dave Carter. *Mountain Biking*. Champaign: Human Kinetics Publishers, 1994.

Editors of Bicycling and Mountain Bike Magazines. *Complete Guide to Bicycle Maintenance and Repair*. Emmaus: Rodale Press, 1994.

Redd, Jim. *The Illinois and Michigan Canal, A Contemporary Perspective in Essays and Photographs*. Carbondale: Southern Illinois University Press, 1993.

Sloane, Eugene A. *Sloan's Complete Book of Bicycling*. 25th Anniversary Edition. New York: Simon & Schuster, 1995.

Van der Plas, Rob. *The Mountain Bike Book*. 3d ed. Mill Valley: Bicycle Books, 1995.

Yeater, Mary M. *The Hennepin Canal*. American Canals. Bulletin of the American Canal Society.

Zyznieuski, Walter G., and George S. Zyznieuski. *Illinois Hiking and Backpacking Trails*. Rev. ed. Carbondale: Southern Illinois University Press, 1993.

WALTER G. ZYZNIEUSKI was born and raised in Illinois. He has traveled the state extensively and has been employed with state and local governments in the environmental field, for the past seventeen years. As a past board member of Rails-to-Trails Conservancy, Illinois chapter, he has been involved with statewide trail-planning activities. He has also coauthored *Illinois Hiking and Backpacking Trails, Revised Edition*, with his brother George. Walter Zyznieuski has an M.A. in Environmental Studies from Sangamon State University and a B.S. from Southern Illinois University at Carbondale.

GEORGE S. ZYZNIEUSKI has been involved in various aspects of operations management for the last twelve years in the Denver area. He is an avid outdoorsman and continues to visit his home state of Illinois. He is the owner of UniWorld Publishing. He has a B.S. degree in industrial technology from Illinois State University and has completed course work for an M.S. degree in energy conservation/alternative energy from Illinois State University.

MIKE ULM has been the state director of the Illinois chapter of the Rails-to-Trails Conservancy since October of 1992. Before joining RTC, he worked as a project manager in the Leaking Underground Storage Tank Section at the Illinois Environmental Protection Agency. In 1991, he researched and wrote *A Guide to Illinois Rail-Trails*, the first rail-trail guidebook for Illinois. In 1994, he coauthored RTC's first regional guidebook, *40 Great Rail-Trails in Michigan, Illinois and Indiana*. Mike has an undergraduate degree in geography from Illinois State University and a masters degree in environmental planning from the University of Illinois at Springfield.